experiences of psychiatrist Elisabeth Kübler-Ross, who has gained wide acclaim for her work with the terminally ill; the studies of near-death experiences conducted by Raymond A. Moody, Jr.

In evaluating the evidence uncovered in each stage of man's continuing scientific investigation of the human soul, Milbourne Christopher makes clear that while there is as yet no absolute scientific proof of out-of-the-body experiences, the search becomes more and more intense and sophisticated.

Someday we may be able to say more about the soul than the primitives who once described it as "invisible as the aroma of a flower and as elusive as the wind." Until then, the search for the soul remains one of man's boldest enterprises, as this new book bears fascinating witness.

Milbourne Christopher is America's leading magician and chairman of the Occult Investigation Committee of the Society of American Magicians. His other books include *ESP, Seers & Psychics,* and *Houdini: Untold Story.* He lives in New York City.

SEARCH FOR THE SOUL

Also by Milbourne Christopher

Houdini: The Untold Story
ESP, Seers & Psychics
The Illustrated History of Magic
Mediums, Mystics & the Occult
Houdini: A Pictorial Life
Milbourne Christopher's Magic Book

Milbourne Christopher

SEARCH
FOR THE
SOUL

THOMAS Y. CROWELL, PUBLISHERS
Established 1834   New York

SEARCH FOR THE SOUL. Copyright © 1979 by Milbourne Christopher. All rights reserved. Printed in the United States of America. No part of this book may be used or reproduced in any manner whatsoever without written permission except in the case of brief quotations embodied in critical articles and reviews. For information address Thomas Y. Crowell, Publishers, 521 Fifth Avenue, New York, N.Y. 10017. Published simultaneously in Canada by Fitzhenry & Whiteside Limited, Toronto.

FIRST EDITION

Designer: Suzanne Haldane

Library of Congress Cataloging in Publication Data

Christopher, Milbourne.
　Search for the soul.

　Includes index.
　1. Psychical research. I. Title.
BP1031.C54　　　133'.07'2　　　78–3298
ISBN 0–690–01760–X

79　80　81　82　83　10　9　8　7　6　5　4　3　2　1

133.07
C55

For Monk and Mary Kay

80-1709

CONTENTS

SEARCH FOR THE SOUL

1.

The Search

The quest for scientific evidence of an inner self—a soul—that survives after the body dies and, possibly, can be temporarily separated from it while a person is living has intensified in recent years. A million-dollar bequest in 1968 from Chester F. Carlson, inventor of the xerography process, enabled the American Society for Psychical Research to maintain a laboratory, to which he had earlier presented a computer and other equipment, and to carry out experiments on a scale not feasible in the past. Another Carlson million permitted the University of Virginia School of Medicine to set up a Division of Parapsychology, headed by a Carlson Professor of Psychiatry, who amasses and assesses worldwide reports of reincarnation.

The $270,000 estate of James Kidd, a missing gold prospector, awarded in 1972 by an Arizona court to the American Society for Psychical Research, financed ASPR field trips to India, where statements about deathbed visions were collected and later compared with those earlier accumulated in the United States. The Kidd bonanza also paid for out-of-the-body studies in the society's Manhattan laboratory and at the Psychical Research Foundation's buildings in Durham, North Carolina. (The latter organization was founded in 1960 for a single purpose—to plan and evaluate soul-survival tests.) In theory, if the consciousness of a living person can be projected to events occurring at a distance, then this is the vital element that continues on after bodily decay. Tantalized by the thought that detached personalities of the living might supplant sensitive, but less far-reaching, surveillance instruments, American intelligence agencies dream of an era of ethereal superspies. Consider the possibilities: An agent sits in a secluded room with a tape recorder by his side, a pad on a table, and a pen in his hand. He sends his awareness through space, penetrating concrete and steel barriers, into the War Room of a hostile nation. Or, speedily and invisibly he enters an underground plant somewhere in Asia to view and sketch atomic weapons being manufactured there.

Such conjectured uses of the soul potential distress psychical researchers. Their goal is to validate an ancient and widespread belief. Pythagoras, Plato, and other ancient thinkers agreed that the soul existed. They differed as to its exact location and size. The head, to some, seemed a logical housing. However, an early Hindu writer declared that the soul was as large as a thumb and could be found in the center of the body.

The soul concept in Egypt was more complicated. Each soul had several parts. One part was a duplicate of the body; another could enter a second person; still another remained with the corpse in its tomb. A fourth fragment held the emotions, while other essential pieces were contained in the shadow of the duplicate body.

Decorations on ancient Grecian urns depict the soul escaping from the mouths of the dying, a concept also accepted in India and Egypt. Stone carvings, woodcuts, and paintings of early Christians show small unclad replicas of the dead emerging from between their open lips and being greeted by angels or demons.

Tibetan Buddhists conceived of death not as the final state, but as the start of a transition of the inner self to a new body. They thought that this passage usually took about fifteen days. Though souls left quietly in Tibet, Homer tells in his *Iliad* of one shrieking faintly on its way to the next world. The souls of Penelope's paramours were noisier, chirping dismally like bats as they followed Mercury to the underworld. Those escorted by Hercules twittered like excited birds.

Soloman Islanders believed that they heard souls whispering in the fields after dark. For the Algonquin Indians of Canada the mournful sounds that came from forests at night were the moans of the dead. Natives of Greenland described souls as soft, without blood, bones, or sinews. Melanesians, in a warmer part of the world, visualized the soul as being dusty gray, like smoke from a fire. If one was glimpsed, it immediately disappeared.

Sumatrans tied the wounds of warriors securely, so that their souls could not slip away. For months after a Congolese tribesman died, his hut was not cleaned; a remnant of the soul might be swept away with the dust. Superstitious peasants in Britain and Europe threw open doors and shutters as the moment of death approached, so that the flight of the soul would not be hampered by manmade obstacles. Germans warned children not to slam doors; disembodied souls were fragile and might be injured.

Lucretius, a Roman philosopher of the first century B.C., noted in the third book of his *De rerum natura* that the soul was formed of much smaller particles than those in water, vapor, or smoke. For primitive tribes in Central America the soul was like the air they breathed, only finer.

A human is defined as "a living soul" in Genesis 2:7. Once "the silver cord be loosed," Ecclesiastes 12:6 explains, "the spirit shall return unto God who gave it." Plutarch, the Greek historian who served as a Delphic priest, refers to a life-sustaining link between flesh and spirit in his account of Aridaeus, who was stunned by a seemingly lethal blow in A.D. 79. Believing himself to be in the afterlife, Aridaeus saw an uncle there who assured him that he was not dead, since the slender line extending to his unconscious body had not been severed.

Spiritualists in mid-nineteenth-century America contended

that, even though the thread between soul and body had been broken, the dead could communicate through spirit mediums and that mediums could manifest a psychic force powerful enough to tilt and lift a heavy table. Dr. Robert Hare, a graduate of Yale and Harvard, professor of chemistry at the University of Pennsylvania, and member of the American Association for the Advancement of Science, lashed out at the "popular madness" of spiritualism in 1853. Before the year ended, the professor, then in his seventies, attended several séances, planning to expose the charlatans who were duping credulous Philadelphians. Instead, the marvels that he witnessed converted him.

Speaking before an assemblage of believers in New York in September 1854, Dr. Hare solemnly declared that he had sat on a dinner table, with his feet not touching the floor, while the table, lifted by a psychic force, beat time to songs being sung in the séance room. The most remarkable medium whom he had met was a boy, the son of a friend. The lad accompanied him on a trip to Canada. En route, in New York, the boy's cap disappeared, but then fell from above when the owner was far away. Keys to their stateroom on a Montreal-bound boat and to the professor's traveling carpetbag vanished one morning. A spirit message relayed by the boy said that the stateroom key was in the locked bag, while the key for the bag was in Dr. Hare's trunk. This information proved to be correct.

While in Montreal, the professor locked several balls, a "spirit-scope," his shaving case, razor strap, and other gear in the carpetbag; then he turned away. Suddenly the balls rained down on him, followed by the other objects. Another day, the key to the bag disappeared again. Later, as Dr. Hare and the young medium were riding through the city streets, the key fell from above and struck the astonished professor on the chest.

Dr. Hare asserted that these strange occurrences were spiritualistic manifestations. Skeptical academic colleagues, however, thought that the distinguished professor had been deceived by the pranks of a youngster. Nonetheless, Hare was the first scientist to conduct a laboratory experiment designed to detect the presence of a psychic force. This and other tests of psychic powers are described in his *Experimental Investigation of the Spirit Manifestations: Demonstrating the Existence of Spirits and Their Communion with Mortals* (1855).

A glass receptacle containing water was fixed to the short side of a plank four feet long and eight inches wide, which was balanced like a seesaw on a fulcrum extending up from a sturdy trestle. A wire colander was suspended from a rigid post into the water-filled, transparent bowl. Hanging down from a tripod on the far side of the fulcrum, spring scales supported the end of the long side of the plank.

Standing close to the plank, Henry C. Gordon, a medium, lowered his clasped hands into the colander in the bowl, not touching either the bottom or the sides. This action had an instant effect on the scales. The seventy-two-year-old professor noted that a three-pound pull had been registered. As the end of the plank supported by the scales was six times farther away from the point of balance than was the bowl, Dr. Hare reported that an eighteen-pound, invisible force had been applied to the portion of the plank attached to the scales. Subsequent experiments with Gordon demonstrated that the intensity of his psychic pressure did not vary.

Testing the boy medium with the same equipment, Dr. Hare observed that the youngster's psychic force was stronger than the adult's. The scales indicated a seven-pound tug—a forty-two pound pressure. In this case, the mysterious impact was so forcible that the equipment toppled over.

The professor also devised several mechanical devices so that mediums could spell out messages from the spirits more rapidly than the Fox sisters, the founders of modern spiritualism. (At the Fox séances letters of the alphabet were called out or pointed to on a board until rapping noises confirmed that the right letters had been reached.)

One of the professor's systems involved a long table with wheels at the ends of the four legs. One front wheel was connected by a long loop to a large disk with letters of the alphabet around its face, placed at the front of the table. A medium sat at the far side of the table, with her hands on a small board supported by metal balls resting on the top of the table. As the table shifted to the left or right, the disk turned, bringing to the top the letters of each word from the afterlife. Portable versions of this instrument were employed when Dr. Hare escorted a medium to other houses for séances.

The *New York Times* reported that three thousand people filled the Broadway Tabernacle when Dr. Hare lectured there on November 23, 1855. In his talk on "Celestial Machinery," the professor described his researches in physics and chemistry as insignificant. The work in which he was now engaged had a far more profound meaning for mankind. Souls survived, and he, through mediums, had been in communication with great personages of the past. He had learned that the spirit body is similar to, but not the same as, the earthly one. Spirits had respiratory and circulatory systems; they breathed, but inhaled something infinitely finer than air.

Physicists and chemists who had welcomed the professor's opinions now shunned him; fellow members of the American Association for the Advancement of Science objected to his attempts to address that body on a subject they thought to be the result of hallucinations. Before he died in 1858, the first scientist to investigate the issue of soul survival became a medium himself, no longer requiring an intermediary for his alleged conversations with the dead.

Not until twelve years later did another eminent chemist and physicist startle his associates with the announcement that he too was investigating a force said to be spiritualistic. William Crookes's researches in London were to be followed by efforts of other probers to photograph, weigh, and measure souls. Harvard philosopher William James and British physicist Sir Oliver Lodge were to testify to the amazing trance communications of Leonora Piper, a Boston medium.

Contemporary investigators, such as Dr. Karlis Osis, Carlson Research Fellow of the American Society for Psychical Research, study new reports of the afterlife from near-death hospital patients and from people who have been resuscitated after being pronounced clinically dead. They also design new out-of-the-body experiments for those who claim that their consciousness has traveled to distant places.

Dr. Elisabeth Kübler-Ross, the Swiss-born psychiatrist who gained fame with her sympathetic and comforting advice to the terminally ill and their families, tells friends about her personal psychic experiences: how she projected her soul far into outer space and was menaced on earth by evil forces.

Dr. Ian Stevenson, Carlson Professor of Psychiatry at the University of Virginia School of Medicine, is more reticent. If he recalls an earlier life himself, he has not discussed it in print, but his scholarly studies of reincarnations make it clear that he considers the evidence for survival in another body to be worthy of serious consideration.

This book offers an account of the efforts that have been made to see, isolate, and analyze the soul. It tells of strange experiments in séance rooms and laboratories more than a hundred years ago and equally intriguing tests utilizing scientific equipment in modern times. It affords the reader an opportunity to compare deathbed visions of another era with those reported or experienced today.

2.

The Soul
in Human Form

Impetuously testing the solidity of a female spirit materialized in a gaslit room, William Crookes, the first British scientist to seek proof that the soul survives after the body dies, took the lovely phantom tenderly in his arms and, in his own words, "did—well, as any gentleman would do under the circumstances." Other distinguished Fellows of the Royal Society who were married and had fathered nine children might have been as daring, but it is most unlikely that they would have described the episode in print, rhapsodizing about the spirit's beauty and quoting from Byron's *Don Juan* to extol her charms.

Spiritualism had been scorned by the most respected members of Britain's scientific community. Michael Faraday, the physicist, scoffed at it as being "utterly contemptible" and without "the least value to mankind." Thomas Henry Huxley, the biologist, termed it "as great an imposture as ever came under my notice."

Crookes disagreed with his colleagues. Long before his encounter with the appealing spirit, he had listed, in the June 5, 1871, issue of the *Spiritualist,* a London weekly, the important questions that a carefully conducted probe might answer: Were there spirits? If so, how could this be proven?

Did they have the same characteristics in the body and after being released from it? Did intelligent spirits issue from the dead, or were they "an order of beings separate from the human race?" Did the dead communicate with the living? Were they striving to send their messages through in some more satisfactory way?

The best qualified investigator, Crookes contended, would be "a man of science, without feeling or sentiment. All romantic and superstitious ideas should be suppressed and he should be guided by hard intellect alone."

He himself had the right scientific background. Born in London in 1832, Crookes mastered laboratory techniques at the Royal College of Chemistry. After working as a meteorologist at the Radcliffe Observatory, Oxford, he instructed classes in chemistry at a college in Chester. Following his marriage to Ellen Humphrey in 1856, he achieved success as an experimental chemist and physicist in his own laboratory in London. He also edited two photography periodicals and in 1859 established the weekly *Chemical News*. Two years later he made news himself when he discovered thallium, a metallic element. This led to his election as a Fellow of the Royal Society and to the editor's chair at the prestigious *Quarterly Journal of Science*.

Crookes became intrigued by psychic phenomena in 1869, several months after a committee appointed by the London Dialectical Society had begun a study of spiritualism. Thomas Huxley, invited to serve as a consultant, had declined, saying that "the only good I can see in a demonstration of the truth of 'Spiritualism' is to furnish an additional argument against suicide. Better live as a crossing-sweeper than die and be made to talk twaddle by a 'medium' hired at a guinea a *séance.*"

The most famous medium to appear before the committee never accepted money for séances, but he did permit his admirers to pay for his travel and living expenses and to present him with expensive jewels. Daniel Dunglas Home, a slender, blue-eyed Scot with abundant hair, a moustache, and a most affable manner, had awed the rulers of Russia,

Prussia, and France, and had enthralled Elizabeth Barrett Browning, Lord Adare, and the Master of Lindsay in England. Adare, the son of the Earl of Dunraven, and Lindsay, whose father was the Earl of Crawford, solemnly testified that Home had floated out through an open window in one room high above the street and then in through another in the adjacent chamber. They and other witnesses assured the Dialectical Society's investigators that they had seen the marvelous medium materialize spirit hands and, on occasion, complete spirit bodies.

Accompanied by his friends Adare and Lindsay, Home arrived to be tested on the evening of April 2, 1869, at the home of a committeeman. He changed clothes in the presence of two witnesses, so that they could see there were no secret devices concealed up his sleeves. Dr. James Edmunds, the chairman, noted that the medium possessed "an extremely muscular and elastic" physique.

The séance, staged in a well-lighted dining room, lasted two hours and twenty minutes. Despite the onlookers' high expectations, no spirit hands or forms materialized. Home did not levitate himself and write on the ceiling, nor did the large table behind which he sat soar up from the floor. The committee report stated that the manifestations "were of the most trifling character, consisting of a few raps and slight movements of the table." After Home and his titled friends left the room, Dr. Edmunds demonstrated how easily the table could be agitated with minimal muscular exertion.

Home presided at three more séances for the committee, with equally disappointing results. The following year, on March 19, 1870, he submitted to another test, in Russia at the University of St. Petersburg. There, as in England, it had been rumored that the spirit hand produced by the medium during private sittings was really one of his feet secretly slipped from his boot beneath a table. Guarding against this possible deception, the Russians seated Home at a table with a transparent glass top—a precaution never taken previously. Aside from the swaying motion of the table and the noises noted by the committee in England, this séance too was a failure.

While Home was away, the Dialectical Society's committee asked William Crookes to attend several séances. He accepted on the proviso that his name not be mentioned and that he not be asked for an opinion. He also had private sittings with some of London's most popular psychics—and was astonished by their incredible feats. In the July 1870 issue of the *Quarterly Journal of Science* Crookes confirmed a report published in the *Athenaeum,* another periodical, that he had started his own investigation. He explained that he was examining spiritualistic phenomena to establish their validity "or to explain, if possible, the delusions of the honest and to expose the tricks of deceivers."

That "the movement of material substances, and the productions of sounds resembling electric discharges, occur under circumstances in which they cannot be explained by any physical law at present known," he stated emphatically, "is a fact of which I am as certain as I am of the most elementary fact in chemistry." As yet, he continued, he had no absolute proof that these manifestations were spiritual in nature. Such evidence "must be so strikingly and convincingly true that we cannot, dare not deny it."

This statement of purpose appealed to both skeptics and believers. Skeptics were sure that the alleged wonders could not withstand scientific scrutiny. Believers noted with pleasure that Crookes had accepted without question the supernormal movements of objects and the rapping sounds that were a part of many séances.

A year later, when Crookes published an account of his "Experimental Investigation of a New Force" in his journal, those who had considered him to be a reliable exponent of scientific methodology began to doubt his ability. Crookes asserted that Daniel Dunglas Home had caused an accordian to play while holding it with one hand in a cage under a table. Why, critics wondered, was this done under a table and not above it in full view? Crookes also claimed that Home had added pounds to the weight of a board suspended between a table and a spring balance by lightly touching the portion on the table. Crookes, critics charged, had not considered the many possibilities of fraud.

Had Home used his foot while Crookes's eyes were on his hand? Had he secretly attached a thin but strong thread to the scales? No precautions against possible deceptions were mentioned.

Crookes summed up his three years of investigation in his "Notes of an Enquiry into the Phenomena called Spiritual" in the January 1874 issue of the *Quarterly Journal of Science.* These notes either documented Crookes's astute observations or, depending upon the reader's attitude, his compulsive desire to believe in the incredible.

The scientist wrote that he had seen Home materialize pale spirit hands on several occasions. Once, after a leaf was removed from the center of a dining-room table, a hand came up through the opening and gave Crookes a flower. Three times, the scientist stated, he had looked on while Home levitated himself. How high the medium ascended or how well the area was illuminated, Crookes did not say.

Twice, phantom forms appeared. One, "dark, shadowy, semitransparent," was glimpsed by a window, "waving the curtain with his hand." The other emerged "from a corner of the room," picked up an accordian, and "then glided about the room playing the instrument." As the specter approached a woman, "she gave a slight cry, upon which it vanished." Apparently there was no time to study these remarkable manifestations scientifically. They came when least expected and disappeared without a trace.

Crookes found Home to be a fascinating dinner guest, even when not communing with the dead. He amused the family with stories of his exploits in Europe and the United States and, before the séances began, often entertained with his skill at the piano.

Another welcome visitor to the scientist's home was Kate Fox. As a child in a Hydesville, New York, farmhouse she and her sister Maggie had produced, on March 31, 1848, the rapping sounds that heralded the birth of modern spiritualism. Escorted by their mother and Leah, a much older, married sister, the girls came to Manhattan two years later. Their séances at Barnum's Hotel attracted such celebrities as William Cullen Bryant, the poet; James Fenimore Cooper, the novelist; and Horace Greeley, the editor of the *Tribune.* The spirits rapped loudly when the answer to a question posed by a sitter was yes and spelled out words by knocking when a client touched the required letters on a printed alphabet card.

In 1860 Kate found a wealthy patron, Charles E. Livermore, a New York banker, then mourning the death of his beloved wife, Estelle. Kate gave 388 séances for him, several of which were described in the excerpts quoted with his permission from his diary in Robert Dale Owen's *The Debatable Land* (1871). For example, as Livermore sat with Kate in the dark on the evening of March 14, 1860, listening to "the spiritual telegraph," he was conscious of a hazy spectral form in the room. Several nights later a luminous globe appeared. He briefly glimpsed his dead wife's face before the manifestation faded away. Eventually the figure as well as the face of Estelle materialized during the séances. One evening Livermore stroked the spirit's hair. It was "identical with human hair," he said, "but, after a brief space, it melted away, leaving nothing in my grasp."

During some of the years that she conducted séances for the banker, Kate lived with the Greeley family. They had arranged for her to further her limited education and learn the niceties of social life when she visited them as a young girl. Unfortunately, as her development as a medium progressed, Kate became an alcoholic. Periodically she tried to abstain, but the urge for intoxication was too strong to resist. Her drinking became so excessive in the fall of 1871 that Livermore decided on a radical change of scene to save her from self-destruction. He booked passage for her on a ship bound for England and sent one of his female relatives with her as a companion.

"For several months," William Crookes wrote in the report on his investigations, "I enjoyed almost unlimited opportunity of testing the various phenomena occurring in the presence of this lady." No one approached her as a producer of rapping sounds, Crookes proclaimed. If she materialized spirit faces and bodies for him, as she had for Livermore, the scientist did not mention this in his summation.

The most exciting phase of Crookes's probe began late in 1873 when Florence Cook, a personable sixteen-year-old medium, came to him for help. William Volckman, a spiritualist who earlier had been a member of the Dialectical Society's committee, had accused her of fraud. During the séance that Volckman attended, Florence had been tied to a chair and concealed from view by an opaque curtain. As she had many times before, the medium produced a spirit form draped in white from behind the barrier.

The spirit, who said that her name was Katie King, walked among the sitters and talked with them. Volckman suddenly took a firm grip on Katie's hand. When she tried to pull away, he threw his arms around her. Someone quickly doused the single low-burning gas jet in the room, and solid male hands, much stronger than Volckman's, yanked the spirit away and hustled her behind the curtain. When the jet was lighted again and the curtain eventually drawn aside, Katie was gone, and Florence was found tied to her chair as before. Volckman, who had had several hairs tugged from his beard in the dark, had been promptly ejected from the room, as sympathetic sitters left their chairs to console the distraught medium.

A report on the fracas appeared in the *Spiritualist* on December 12, 1873, under the heading "Gross Outrage at a Spirit Circle." Volckman explained his actions in *The Medium and Daybreak,* another periodical, two weeks later. "Having for forty minutes carefully observed and scrutinized the face, features, gestures, size, style and peculiarities of utterance of the so-called spirit, the conviction irresistibly forced itself upon me that *no ghost,* but the medium, Miss Florence Cook herself, was before the circle." He charged that she had walked on her toes to create the illusion that Katie King was taller, and he had been struck by "the utter puerility of her remarks."

In the December 29, 1894, issue of *Light,* another spiritist periodical, Florence wrote, "I went to Mr. Crookes myself . . . and offered myself a willing sacrifice on the altar of his disbelief. It was immediately after the unpleasant incident of Mr. Volckman, and those who did not understand said many cruel things of me." Crookes had been criticized for his endorsement of the phenomena exhibited by Daniel Dunglas Home and Kate Fox. When the forty-one-year-old Fellow of the Royal Society championed the cause of the pretty teenage medium, more eyebrows were raised in amazement.

Crookes stated unequivocally that he had heard the moans of Florence Cook come from behind a curtain while Katie King stood in front of it. Katie seemed to be "startlingly life-like and real" and her "features resembled those of Miss Cook," but the sounds from the far side of the barrier indicated to him that the spirit was a separate entity. The medium had for weeks been sitting only for Crookes and his friends. "Let those who are inclined to judge Miss Cook harshly, suspend their judgement until I bring forward positive evidence which I think will be sufficient to settle the question," he cautioned in a letter published in the February 6, 1874, issue of the *Spiritualist.*

The scientist sent "absolute proof" to the April 3 edition of the weekly. On March 12 Katie King, after chatting with the sitters, went behind the curtain that hung between his laboratory and his library. A minute later she called for him to come to the library and put the medium's head back on a sofa, from which it was dangling down at one side. Crookes responded immediately and "in spite of the darkness" could see that Florence was still in her black velvet frock and not in a white spirit costume.

He returned to his chair in the laboratory. Soon Katie came forward, telling him to extinguish the gas jet and pick up his lamp—a bottle containing phosphorized oil, which, when uncorked, emitted a glow. She held the open bottle close to her face, gave it back, and again invited him to the far side of the curtain. Crookes said that the medium was still on the sofa, but that Katie had disappeared. She reappeared to tell him that she had been near the medium as he bent over her.

The only thing proved by this tale, the doubter will say, was that Crookes was more gullible than ever. If he ever suspected that the teenage medium was deceiving him with her skillful maneuvering, this suspicion was dispelled on the evening of March 29, during a séance at Florence Cook's home in Hackney, a suburb of London. "Katie never appeared to greater perfection," Crookes enthused. For almost two hours the spirit had been visible talking with the sitters. "On several occasions she took my arm when walking and the impression conveyed to my mind that it was a living woman by my side, instead of a visitor from the other world, was so strong that the temptation to repeat a recent celebrated experiment became almost irresistible. . . ."

Asking for and receiving permission to embrace Katie, he took her in his arms and "did—well, as any gentleman would do under the circumstances." This action enabled him to establish that she "was as material a being as Miss Cook herself." Katie, he added, did not struggle to get away, as she had when William Volckman had clutched her.

Then Katie told the scientist to turn out the gas jet, take his corked phosphorous lamp, and come with her into the room beyond the drapes. Proceeding "cautiously" in the dark, Crookes felt about with his free hand until he touched the medium. She was "crouching on the floor." He pulled the cork from the bottle and by the glow saw, as he knelt, Florence Cook in her black gown.

She did not flinch as he took one of her hands in his and moved the light nearer her face. Turning his head, raising the lamp, and glancing at Katie King, he satisfied himself that she was the lovely spirit he had held shortly before and not "the phantasm of a disordered brain." He carefully examined the medium three times to be sure that she was "a living woman" and three times scanned Katie—until I had no doubt of her objective reality." When the spirit signaled for him to leave the medium's side, he obeyed. Katie vanished. He stayed in the dark until the medium revived and two people "came in with a light."

He wrote that he had studied the spirit and the medium almost simultaneously, and he emphasized the differences between them. Katie was taller by four and a half inches. Katie's "skin was perfectly smooth both to touch and sight": Florence had a large blister on her neck. Katie's ears were unblemished; Florence's had been pierced for earrings. Katie's complexion was light; Florence's was dark. Katie had a fuller face and longer fingers than the medium. This and the previous séance were reported by Crookes to the *Spiritualist* on March 30, 1874.

Delighted by the results of his experiments with Florence Cook, Crookes invited another teenage medium to his house. Mary Showers, also a specialist in full-form materializations, was a friend of Florence's. The spirit she produced also was named Florence.

"Miss Cook's 'Katie' has been walking about in my laboratory along with Miss Showers's 'Florence' with their arms entwined schoolgirl fashion, and in a strong light. 'Katie' has also materialized and spoken when I have been in the cabinet [his library] with Miss Cook, holding her hand." It was so dark, he continued, that he "could see nothing except lights here and there, one of which settled on my coat-sleeve." Crookes was quoted in the April 10, 1874, issue of the *Spiritualist* on what happened when the two young psychics became entranced at the same time.

Strange activities for an eminent scientist. Not as strange, however, as happenings still to come. Edward W. Cox, a lawyer, believer in psychic phenomena, and one of Crookes's friends, did not approve of schoolgirl shenanigans. In the *Spiritualist* dated May 15, 1874, he wrote that he had seen the prankish spirits, Katie and Florence, "playing girlish tricks, patting us and pushing us. . . . They breathed, and perspired, and ate, and wore a white head-dress and a white robe from neck to foot, made of cotton and woven by a loom." They not only resembled the mediums, "they were facsimiles of them." It would be easy, Cox suggested, to settle the matter. If the curtain were left unclosed as the spirits draped in white cavorted, the entranced mediums also could be seen. Then and only then could investigators be sure there had been no deception.

Cox offered eye-witness evidence that Mary Showers cheated. He had been at a séance when Florence, the alleged spirit, put her shrouded head through the drapes. An inquisitive woman sitter, perhaps not realizing that she was violating the rules of séance etiquette, pulled the curtain aside. The chair in which the medium had been seated was empty. Mary, masquerading as the spirit, was standing wearing a "ghost head-dress" and the black frock that she had been seen in earlier. Until this unexpected intrusion Mary had had her eyes rolled upward. They quickly focused on the interloper, and the medium tried desperately to tug the drapes together with her hands. The head covering toppled off during the struggle and fell to the floor.

"You have killed my medium," the "spirit" shrieked—a cry still heard when a callous skeptic suddenly flashes a light during a sitting in a dark room. The medium did not lose her life, Cox reported, just some of her composure. She claimed that she had been entranced and not conscious of her duplicity.

Crookes may have had second thoughts about the mediumship of Mary Showers after this exposure, but he still seemed to have complete confidence in the integrity of Florence Cook. One night he took Katie King's pulse. "It beat steadily at seventy-five, whilst Miss Cook's pulse a little time after, was going at its usual rate of ninety," he reported. "On applying my ear to Katie's chest I could hear a heart beating rhythmically inside, and pulsating even more steadily than did Miss Cook's when she allowed me to try a similar experiment after the *séance.*" He also determined that the lungs of the spirit were in better condition than those of the medium, "for at the time I tried my experiment Miss Cook was under treatment for a severe cough."

Photography, Crookes pronounced after using five cameras

to make more than forty pictures of the spirit, had been "inadequate to depict the perfect beauty of Katie's face." He quoted from Byron—deleting (as writer Trevor Hall noted in *The Spiritualists* in 1962) two lines about purity—in an attempt to express the emotions she aroused in him.

> Round her she made an atmosphere of life,
> The very air seemed lighter from her eyes,
> They were so soft and beautiful, and rife
> With all we can imagine of the skies:
> Her overpowering presence made you feel
> It would not be idolatry to kneel.

The final, and in many ways the most memorable, appearance of Katie King at a Florence Cook séance occurred the night of May 21, 1874, at the medium's home. Crookes's account of that event appeared fifteen days later in the *Spiritualist.* From notes made at the time, he cited a part of Katie's farewell address. "Mr. Crookes has done very well throughout, and I leave Florrie with the greatest confidence in his hands, feeling perfectly sure he will not abuse the trust I place in him. He can act in an emergency better than I can myself, for he has more strength."

Following the spirit, at her request, into the room behind the drapes, Crookes apparently could see in the dark. Katie, he said, stooped down, touching the medium, and called, "Wake up, Florrie, wake up! I must leave you now." Regaining consciousness, the medium wept and pled with the spirit to delay her departure.

"My dear, I can't; my work is done. God bless you," Katie answered. At the spirit's suggestion Crookes supported the medium, who was sobbing "hysterically." When he turned toward the spirit again, "the white-robed Katie had gone." After the medium had calmed down, "a light was procured," and Crookes escorted her out from behind the curtain.

The spirit's final séance appearance was described in the same issue of the *Spiritualist* by another witness, Florence Marryat (Mrs. Ross Church), a popular novelist, platform personality and sometime diva, who had been among the friends invited by Florence Cook to see Katie King's final bow. Katie, the novelist said, gave each of her admirers "a bouquet of flowers tied up with a ribbon, a piece of her dress and veil, and a note which she wrote with her pencil before us."

Summoned behind the curtain for a private farewell before Katie returned to the spirit land, the sitters one by one went to the far side of the barrier. Despite the darkness, Florence Marryat "again saw and touched the warm breathing body of Florence Cook lying on the floor, and then stood upright by the side of Katie, who desired me to place my hands inside the loose single garment which she wore and feel her nude body. I did so thoroughly."

Crookes, it should be mentioned, admitted that his own report was complete only "as far as I can publish it." Seventeen years later, in *There Is No Death,* a lurid memoir of her adventures, Miss Marryat had more to say about the spirit and the scientist, "who was as attached to her as she was to him." She claimed that she had been one of the sitters when Crookes made the tests referred to in his book *Researches in the Phenomena of Spiritualism* (1874), a collection of his articles. She fantasized that she had "seen Florrie's dark curls *nailed down to the floor,* outside the curtain, in view of the audience," while Katie strolled and conversed with those present. The novelist said that, before Katie materialized, the medium weighed 112 pounds on Crookes's weighing device behind the curtain, but only half as much after the spirit body formed.

One night, while Katie was sitting on her lap, Florence Marryat realized that the spirit was perspiring. Asked whether, at least for the moment, she had nerves, lungs, veins, and the other essential parts of a living person, the spirit replied, "I have everything that Florrie has." To prove this, she invited her friend behind the curtain, dropped her white robe, and "stood perfectly naked."

"Now," Katie stated, "you can see that I am a woman." Not just a female, the novelist stressed, but "a most beautifully made woman . . . and I examined her well." Florence

Marryat sat on the floor by the entranced medium, as the spirit had instructed; Katie knelt and kissed her. "Where is your dress, Katie?" the writer inquired. The nude spirit replied, "Oh, that's gone, I've sent it on before me." Told to strike a match and light a candle after Katie had knocked three times, the novelist complied. As the match burst into flame, Katie evaporated "like a flash of lightning."

This instant disappearance, while awe-inspiring, was not as amazing as the spirit's spectacular disintegration at another séance attended by the novelist. Confessing that she could not withstand the glare of intense light, Katie stood with her back to a wall, her arms outstretched and pressed against it.

> Then the gas-burners were turned on to their full extent. . . . She began gradually to melt away. I can compare the dematerialization of her form to nothing but a wax doll melting before a hot fire. First, the features became blurred and indistinct; they seemed to run into each other. The eyes sunk in the sockets, the nose disappeared, the frontal bone fell in. Next the limbs appeared to give way under her, and she sank lower and lower on the carpet like a crumbling edifice. At last there was *nothing but her head* left above the ground— then a heap of white drapery only, which disappeared with a whisk, as if a hand had pulled it after her—and we were left staring by the light of three gas-burners at the spot on which "Katie King" had stood.

Florence Marryat wrote the sort of fantastic stories that many readers enjoy; this book is still in print. The melting and disintegration of Katie King occurred only in her imagination.

Did Crookes really believe that Katie King had returned from the dead? From his accounts of the Florence Cook séances one would suppose that he did. Yet on August 1, 1874, a few months after he had seen Katie for the last time, he wrote a letter to a woman in St. Petersburg, Russia, that included these pertinent paragraphs:

> To 'fix the identity of a deceased person' has been the chief object I have had before me for the last three or four years, and I have neglected no opportunity myself on that point. I

had almost unlimited opportunities of investigation, more so perhaps than any other man in Europe. Mr. Home has scarcely given a seance in England during his recent visits without my presence at it, and most of his seances have been at my home or my brother's. For six months Kate Fox was giving seances at my home once or twice a week, and since Christmas last Miss Cook has been almost one of the family, being here more than at her parents' house, and giving tests and seances several times a week. In addition to these highly-gifted mediums I have had frequent seances with all the other good mediums whose names are familiar to Spiritualists. During this whole time I have most earnestly desired to get the one proof you seek—the proof that the dead can return and communicate. . . . I have never once had satisfactory proof that this is the case. . . . I know how earnestly the soul craves for one little sign of life beyond the grave.

These words were not put into print until twenty-six years later. They appeared in the May 12, 1900, issue of *Light,* a London weekly that usually presented an affirmative view on survival.

In 1875, less than a year after the last known Florence Cook séance at Crookes's home, another young and attractive medium came to him for aid. The feats with which Annie Eva Fay, an American, amazed large and enthusiastic audiences in a concert hall on Portland Square had been replicated by John Nevil Maskelyne and George Alfred Cooke, "The Royal Illusionists and Anti-Spiritists," at Egyptian Hall on Piccadilly. Nevertheless Crookes vouched for her psychic ability and though it was too late for this to do any good in England, she advertised in other countries that she had been endorsed not only by this distinguished Fellow of the Royal Society, but by the Royal Society itself.

Crookes had announced at the start of his probe that he hoped to validate psychic phenomena or to explain the deceptions of charlatans who professed to have supernormal powers. While he did not reveal how trickery could have been employed by the mediums he investigated, some of his friends did. Daniel Dunglas Home, the medium whom Crookes esteemed above all others, lashed out at his less adept competitors in his *Lights and Shadows of Spiritualism* (1877), charging that "the form of fraud most in vogue is the simulation of a spirit form or forms." Home quoted from a letter that Edward W. Cox had sent him. Cox, one of the most active investigators of the period, had seen the written description of the materialization technique prepared by one medium for another.

The medium who wrote the instructions said that she wore a dress that could be removed quickly. Two undergarments were beneath it. Also concealed from view was "a thin muslin veil," folded into a small package. Opened out, the veil was large enough to cover her body. A pocket handkerchief wound around her head and fastened under the chin with a pin altered the shape of her face and hid her hair.

Once behind the protective curtain and thought to be entranced, she rapidly removed her dress, pinned the handkerchief in place, and draped the veil over her head and shoulders. Then she arranged the dress around the pillows of a sofa to give the impression that a woman was there—should a sitter see the form as she came forward.

Cox noted that many people had wondered how a medium could smuggle the white veiling material in and out of a séance room. The medium's instructions had supplied the answer: "It is carried *in her drawers!*" Home mentioned another way to conceal the compressed muslin. It could be hidden behind a sofa before a séance began. Then the medium could be searched without fear of detection. Not wishing to alienate the famous scientist who had endorsed him, Home added that "the carefully-conducted experiments of Mr. Crookes and Miss Cook were repaid by evidence giving undeniable certainty of the phenomena." Though two chapters of Home's book explained how fraudulent psychics exhibited their counterfeit miracles, there was no hint that the spirit raps heard by Crookes when Home or Kate Fox was present could be made by humans.

Eleven years later, however, Kate and her sister Maggie

told reporters in New York that spiritualism had ruined their lives and those of thousands of others. The sisters appeared at the Academy of Music on October 21, 1888. Onstage, Maggie slipped her right foot from her shoe and put it on top of a low stand. Looking at the back of the crowded hall, she created the illusion that the famous raps came from there. Then by directing her eyes first to the walls and then to the stand, as the sounds became progressively louder, she made it appear that the knocks followed her gaze. Two doctors by her side could see no movement of her foot, though she confessed that she was snapping her big toe. When they touched the foot, they could feel the muscular movement.

Despite this revelation, Crookes continued his search for proof that the soul survives. Elected president of the Society for Psychical Research in 1896, he served three terms. Knighted by Queen Victoria in 1897, he became the president of the British Association for the Advancement of Science the following year.

In his inaugural speech before the British Association Crookes said, "No incident in my scientific career is more widely known than the part I took many years ago in certain psychic researches. To ignore the subject would be an act of cowardice—an act of cowardice I feel no temptation to commit." He regretted "only a certain crudity" in his reports, "which, no doubt justly, militated against their acceptance by the scientific world."

These investigations, he said, were the most important he had made, but if he were starting them anew, he would begin with another phase of phenomena—telepathy. "Steadily, unflinchingly, we strive to pierce the inmost heart of Nature. . . . Veil after veil we have lifted, and her face grows more beautiful, august, and wonderful, with every barrier that is withdrawn."

The brilliant laboratory analyst's discoveries in the fields of radiation and chemistry won him the coveted Order of Merit in 1910. Acceptable evidence that the barrier between life and death had been penetrated continued to elude him.

In December 1916, six months after the death of his wife,

Crookes traveled to Crewe for a séance with William Hope, a spirit photographer. Faces of the dead, and sometimes messages from them, appeared on the pictures he took of the living as they sat in front of his camera. (William H. Mumler had devised the double-exposure technique in Boston in 1862.) On one of the plates that the eighty-four-year-old scientist brought with him and was permitted to develop himself, several scrawled words addressed to his friend Sir Oliver Lodge materialized. On another an unmistakable likeness of his dead wife appeared by his side.

Crookes wrote Lodge that "this definite proof of survival" had lessened his sorrow. Lodge, though a firm believer in psychic phenomena, replied that he had found Hope to be unworthy of trust. Crookes was not to be dissuaded. He said that he had studied the methods of fraudulent spirit photographers years earlier and could vouch for the authenticity of this picture. He vouched for it again the year before he died, in the December 4, 1918, issue of *Christian Commonweal.*

As a member of the Ghost Club, a group of men who met for dinner and told about their eerie experiences, Crookes sent the club what he considered to be "unimpeachable" evidence that his wife had survived and revealed to them that he had heard her voice. Visitors to the College of Psychic Studies in London can still see a print of the photograph that Hope made of the scientist and his spirit wife. The typed caption, "Presented to the Ghost Club at the request of my Wife, speaking in direct voice after her entry into Spirit Life," is followed by the great scientist's signature. Was this proof of survival, to quote Crookes's specification of 1874, "so striking and convincingly true that we cannot, dare not deny it?"

Five years and two months after William Hope had convinced Crookes that photographs of the dead could be taken, Hope came to London for a series of séances at the College of Psychic Science (now the College of Psychic Studies). On the morning of February 24, 1922, Harry Price, a member of the Society for Psychical Research as well as the Magicians Club of London and the Society of American Magicians, arrived at the college for a sitting with the medium. As Crookes had done earlier, Price carried with him a package of photographic plates. These plates, however, had been secretly marked by the manufacturer. The X-ray-imposed emblem of the firm—a crowned, rampant lion and a scroll bearing the word "Imperial"—would be seen only when the plates were developed.

"Nearer My God to Thee" and other hymns were sung, and Hope prayed; then he escorted his client into a darkroom. Following the medium's instructions, Price inserted two of his plates into a camera slide. Hope took the slide, telling Price to close and tie the box containing the remaining plates. Unlike the usual sitter, Price did not look down at the box; he kept his eyes on the medium. There was enough light coming through a red window for Price to see Hope step back, swing partially around, and, apparently, switch the loaded slide with another one that had been in the upper left pocket of his coat.

After Hope placed the slide in his camera in the adjacent room, Price posed for him. Then Price was permitted to develop the two plates himself. A woman's face, as well as his own likeness, appeared on one of the plates. The lion emblem did not become visible on either.

That afternoon, Price, Eric J. Dingwall, research officer of the Society for Psychical Research, and another member of the society went to the Southampton Row photographic studio of Reginald Haines. The lion symbol appeared when the two unused plates were developed. Obviously Hope had earlier exposed a portion of his own unmarked plate to produce the alleged spirit. An account of this investigation was published in the May issue of the Society for Psychical Research's *Journal*.

If, as Sir William Crookes believed, the dead do return, perhaps he, his wife, and Katie King were sad, silent, and unseen spectators on the occasions when William Hope, using double exposures, attempted to convince more observant investigators than Crookes that he had succeeded in photographing the soul in human form.

3.

The Soul
through a Lens

Spirit photographs of the sort that convinced Sir William Crookes that his dead wife had manifested her presence are still being made today. Sometimes the images are clear, but often they are hazy. The spirits wear clothes, and if in their previous life their vision was poor, they are frequently portrayed in glasses. Amateur photographers who forget to advance the film in their cameras have taken "spirit" photographs accidentally.

The first known attempt to use an optical instrument to view a soul as it emerged from a dying body was made in the United States before the turn of the century. A sensational story in the Chicago *Tribune* reported that the experiment proved, "beyond the possibility of doubt, the existence of a human soul." Headed THE FLIGHT OF A SOUL, it told of a discovery so fantastic that the correspondent in Lincoln, Nebraska, "hesitated to give the circumstances to the public."

Concealing the identity of the researcher at his request, the writer referred to him as Mr. Holland and described him as being small in stature, with gentle eyes and a "thoughtful countenance." Holland, a Christian, believed that souls were duplicates of the bodies they inhabited, but too vaporish for the naked eye to see. He had constructed a viewing device similar in size and shape to a studio camera, through which he thought that he might be able to observe a soul as it ascended from a dying person and took form.

The idea had come to Holland as he listened to an amputee complain about an ache in a foot that was no longer there. Purchasing the most powerful lenses that he could find, Holland installed them in a box covered at the back with an opaque black cloth. After examining "the microbes in the air," Holland persuaded a friend, whose arm had been amputated, to assist him in a preliminary test. Telling the man to imagine that he was tracing letters and words with the index finger of his missing hand, Holland peered through the lenses and saw the hazy duplicate of the lost arm and the movements made by the finger.

To his friend's complete astonishment and his own satisfaction, Holland correctly called out each letter and word. Families of dying persons, however, would not permit the researcher to set up his equipment. Doctors and nurses barred him from hospital rooms where terminally ill patients were housed. A year passed as Holland searched for a subject whose final moments he could study through his magnifying instrument.

Then by chance he entered a courtroom as the case of a penniless vagrant was being heard. The vagrant, a young man in his early twenties, had traveled to Lincoln from an eastern state in the hope that the fresher Nebraskan air would be beneficial to his health. A consumptive disease had sapped his strength. Unable to find work because of his weakened condition, he could no longer support himself.

The judge was about to commit the prisoner to the county poorhouse when Holland stood up and asked permission to approach the bench. He volunteered to take the stranger to his house and to provide him with good food and nursing care. The magistrate complimented Holland on his benevolence, and released the prisoner in his custody.

As Holland had suspected by the man's sallow face and haggard appearance, the disease was approaching its final stage. When it became obvious that death was only hours

away, Holland sent for the Chicago *Tribune* correspondent
and told him the story to this point, explaining that he wanted
a reliable witness to the experiment that he had waited so
long to make.

Holland's wife had nursed the sufferer through the previous night. At 10 o'clock that morning, the experimenter took
her place in the chair by the low bedstead. The reporter
sat a few feet away. The only sound in the room was produced
by the patient's breathing. When it became more labored,
Holland threw open the curtains at the window, so that the
bright rays of the summer sun fell directly on the bed. Next
he wheeled his magnifying device from a corner, added a
supplementary twelve-inch lens at the back, and focused it
carefully. Then he returned to his chair.

Ninety minutes dragged by before a sudden shudder shook
the body on the bed as the man died. "Now is the time,"
Holland whispered to the reporter, whom he signaled to join
him as he lifted the black cloth. Together they looked through
the instrument. The reporter described the scene:

Particles of dust in the air were magnified several thousand
times, and for a time their motion kept a perfect dazzle on
the glass. Then as vapor gathers into clouds, so an object
appeared to be forming a foot above the body on the bed.
Particle seemed to seek particle, as by some molecular attraction, until an object was clearly distinguishable. It seemed
like the vapory form of a man rapidly assuming a more perfect
shape, pure and colorless as the most delicate crystal.

There was a moment of awful stillness, and a feeling came
over me which I can never describe. We bent our eyes intently
upon the glass until, particle by particle, the shapely form
of a man had formed and lay floating a foot above the bed,
moored to the body by a slender cord of its own formation.
The eyes were closed, and the new-formed being seemed
as if it were asleep.

Presently, the cord that held it to the clay parted, and a
gentle tremor passed through the beautiful form—beautiful
indeed, for every limb was of the most perfect mould, such
as earth never beheld.

The eyes of the spirit opened, and a ray of intelligence

and of unspeakable joy passed over its face. It arose to a standing position, and cast one sorrowful look at the tenantless clay that lay so still.

I stepped from behind the darkened apparatus and looked toward the spot where I knew the form was standing, but I beheld nothing. The earth reeled beneath me; I cried out, and fell fainting to the floor. When I again became conscious Mr. Holland was bending over me; his face was of ashen paleness.

This, the first known soul experiment with a magnifying instrument to be reported, has not been cited in surveys dealing with survival. It might have been forgotten had it not been reprinted in *Heart Secrets Revealed; or, Mind-Reading Made Easy*, a rare, undated paperback in the author's collection.

The soul formation and separation process detailed by the Nebraskan writer is very similar to the one described by Andrew Jackson Davis, a pioneer American trance medium. In *The Great Harmonia* (1852) Davis wrote that he saw a spirit body more perfect than the original materialize above the head of a dying woman. When the "umbilical cord" broke, the spirit form descended. The Chicago *Tribune* correspondent in Lincoln fainted before he learned what eventually happened to the spirit body. Davis noted that the one he had seen left the room through an open door en route to the hereafter.

Davis also wrote about the materialization of a soul in his *Death and the After-Life* (1865). It is not known whether the reporter in Nebraska had read or heard about these accounts before his eerie bedside experience. Was the vision he described a hallucination? An actuality and a hallucination are almost identical, psychologists say, except that the former really occurs and the latter only seems to.

A Mr. G. vividly described another deathbed scene in the *Journal of the Society for Psychical Research* in 1902. Three large puffs of smoke floated in from an adjacent room. Mr. G., thinking that the attending physician and friends of the family were there smoking cigars, went to object; the room was empty. The clouds drifted to the bed and obscured it. Peering intently into the mist, Mr. G. discerned the transparent, gold-hued form of a woman, approximately three feet tall. She was wearing flowing robes and a crown. Two other forms clad in white drapery were kneeling and less distinct. In the air above his dying wife, extended horizontally, and moored by a cord attached to her forehead above her left eye was a perfectly shaped, unadorned spirit body.

For five hours Mr. G. watched the spectral form writhe and struggle to release itself. Other people entering the room were not aware of the frenzied action. From time to time Mr. G. told the attending physician, "Doctor, I am going insane." Attempts to dispel the apparition by talking with others who were present, by looking away from the bed, or by shutting his eyes "failed to destroy the illusion." Until his wife died, the image persisted. Then, instantly the spirit body, the spectral trio, and the mist dissolved.

It is one thing to imagine puffs of smoke near a dying person, quite another to photograph them, as Dr. Hippolyte Baraduc, a French physician and student of the occult, did in Paris in 1907. Through his studies of neurology, gynecology, and psychic phenomena, Dr. Baraduc became convinced that invisible radiations from human bodies could be detected and monitored by a biometer, an instrument that he constructed for this purpose. He interpreted the readings as an aid in the diagnosis of illnesses.

Later, with special photographic equipment, he took what he called thought pictures. Anger was indicated by tornado-like spirals; pleasant thoughts produced symmetrical patterns. Despite Baraduc's efforts to interest the French Academy of Medicine in this procedure, it was never accepted for serious consideration.

Dr. Baraduc told about his after-death experiments in *Les morts et leurs manifestations* (1908). He wrote that he had communicated telepathically with his young son André for several years; occasionally André's astral double or soul had left its physical counterpart and returned. When André became consumptive, neither medicine nor spiritual treatments could cure him. Two visits to the shrine at Lourdes did not alleviate his suffering.

André died at the age of nineteen in April 1907, at 9:45 in the morning. Nine hours later his father set up lighting equipment and his camera near the open coffin. (It was not uncommon during this period for photographs to be taken of the dead.) On the print made from the first plate to be exposed, strange irregular patterns were seen. Some resembled tiny, snow-covered fir trees.

Six months later Nadine Baraduc, the physician's wife, died. This time the camera and lights were in position. She sighed three times as she expired, and three balls of light were seen by her husband as he took the initial picture. On the finished print they appear to be fluffy bits of absorbent cotton. Two of the mysterious spheres seem to be merging into one on a subsequent print.

After the funeral, balls of light materialized in various rooms of his house, Dr. Baraduc wrote. Determined to communicate in some way with the psychic force that controlled this phenomenon, the physician held a pen in his hand above a sheet of paper. The hand seemingly moved and wrote on its own volition. The message was that the soul of his wife was imprisoned in the luminous sphere. Eventually, it continued, the thin strands that bound her to this life would break, and he would see her spirit body before it entered the afterlife.

Later, as he gazed on her astral form, it dissolved, and nothing remained but his memories. Some students of the occult maintain that the balls of light in the photographs taken by Dr. Baraduc have never been adequately explained. There is, however, a plausible explanation in Hereward Carrington's *Laboratory Investigations into Psychic Phenomena* (1939).

A photograph had been taken of Carrington's laboratory in New York—not during an experiment, but to show his scientific equipment. A strange ball of light appeared in the picture, though the photographer had not noticed it in the room. For five years Carrington and his associates tried to solve the mystery. There had been no flaw in the film. The luminous spot was not the result of an accident during the developing or printing. Then a photograph of a Carnegie laboratory in Washington, D.C., one not involved with psychic research, was printed in the *Physical Review,* a scientific periodical.

On this photograph was a similar ball of light. Noting this, Carrington realized that a natural cause he had not previously considered might have been responsible for the baffling glow. He enlarged the pertinent portions of the photographs of his laboratory and the one in Washington. Examining the balls of light under a magnifying glass, he found that they were almost indentical.

In each case the luminous spheres were reflections of lights on the camera side of the room striking reflective surfaces that scattered the rays. A comparison of the illustrations in Carrington's book with the ones in Dr. Baraduc's volume indicates that the mysterious balls of light in the French photographs came from a similar source.

Today, people with vivid imaginations, especially those who have read books on psychical phenomena and lurid stories in tabloids, continue to "see" souls rising from dead bodies and to believe that balls of light and ghostly images in photographs are proofs of a psychic force, which in time, they say, will be validated by scientists.

4.

Weighers of Souls

Aside from the dying patients who had volunteered to be his subjects, few people in the Massachusetts General Hospital knew that Dr. Duncan MacDougall had attempted to weigh their souls. He had not discussed his plans with the authorities at the Boston medical center. The public was not aware that he had made the first scientific soul-weighing experiments on record until he published a report on his findings in the May 1907 issue of the *Journal of the American Society for Psychical Research.*

"If personal continuity after the event of bodily death is a fact," the physician wrote in his "Hypothesis Concerning Soul Substance, Together with Experimental Evidence of the Existence of Such Substance," it must occupy a space in the body. To deny this "would be equivalent to thinking that nothing had become or was something, that emptiness had personality, that space itself was more than space, all of which are contradictions and absurd."

Dr. MacDougall rejected the concept advanced by some philosophers that the soul was etheric. Arguing that ether did not exist "in separate masses" and emphasizing that consciousness was highly individual, he decided that the soul substance was either a solid, a liquid, or a gas. Unlike ether, all of these were weighable. If with a measuring instrument he could detect a sudden, inexplicable loss of matter at the time of death, the amount lost would be, he theorized, the weight of a soul.

Dr. MacDougall knew that other medical men might not endorse his project. He noted that half a century earlier, at the 1854 Congress of Physiologists in Göttingen, Germany, not one of the several hundred participants had been willing to discuss the possibility of a soul substance with a delegate named Richard Wagner.

Anubis, the jackal-headed soul escorter of Egyptian legend, held balances for esoteric rites in the afterlife. Dr. MacDougall employed a more complicated device for his research with the dying—a bed mounted on a frame supported by sturdy platform beam scales "sensitive to two-tenths of an ounce."

Weeks before their deaths, the physician assured the patients who volunteered for the tests that they would be given constant care and would experience no added pain. Bypassing those whose final contortions might upset the delicate balance of the scales, Dr. MacDougall chose a man weakened by tuberculosis as his first subject.

The moribund patient was transferred to the bed on the scales. He lost weight slowly, an ounce each hour. This could be explained, the physician said, by the gradual evaporation of the moisture produced by respiration and perspiration. The moment that the patient succumbed, after three hours and forty minutes of observation, the beam end of the scales dropped, hitting the metal bar beneath it with a clang. This sudden and unexplained fall indicated to Dr. MacDougall that the first soul to be monitored weighed precisely three-quarters of an ounce.

To make sure that the man's final gasp had not jarred the beam, the physician, once the body had been removed, stretched out on the bed himself. Inhaling as much air as his lungs could hold, he forcibly expelled it. Then a colleague took his place, huffing and puffing violently. Their exertions caused not the slightest tremor on the scales.

The second patient to be carried to the bed on the scales, a man wracked by consumption, remained practically motionless. Since he did not breathe as rapidly as his predecessor, less moisture was involved; the evaporation rate per hour decreased to three-quarters of an ounce. When, after four hours, respiration ended, the facial muscles continued to twitch. Fifteen minutes later, at the instant of the final convulsion, the beam dropped, signaling the loss of half an ounce. Three minutes after this the heart stopped beating, and another weight loss was recorded—a total of an ounce and a half and fifty grains in eighteen minutes.

The two subjects had been of different temperaments, Dr. MacDougall wrote. He also admitted that he did not know the exact time of death in the second test.

The third patient, like the first, was dying of tuberculosis. His soul substance, like the second subject's, seemed to leave in sections—half an ounce at death, then another full ounce minutes afterward. The physician-researcher did not speculate on these two-part variations.

A fourth case was inconclusive because the patient, a woman in a diabetic coma, died before the scales could be adjusted. Also, in Dr. MacDougall's words, "there was a good deal of interference by people opposed to our work." Despite the unspecified nature of this opposition, the beam had dropped. From three-eighths to half an ounce of lifting power had been applied to return the beam to the position it had occupied when it fell. Dr. MacDougall wrote in his report that he considered this test to be without value.

A weight loss of approximately three-eighths of an ounce was recorded when the fifth patient, another victim of tuberculosis, expired. Curiously, when the beam was raised to the before-death level, it did not lower immediately. About fifteen minutes went by before it sank back to the moment-of-death position.

Dr. MacDougall reported that the final experiment "was not a fair test." The sixth patient died less than five minutes after being taken to the special bed, while the physician was still trying to adjust the beam. A loss of an ounce and a half was noted. However, the test had been conducted so quickly that "an accidental shifting of the sliding weight on the beam" may have accounted for this.

By his own admission, Dr. MacDougall considered only four of the six tests as being worthy of attention. Yet he had been convinced that a strange substance left the body at death and that the human soul could be weighed.

Wondering whether animals had souls, the physician also experimented with dogs. Perfect subjects, he held, would be those so weakened by disease that they could not struggle. Unable to find canines of this sort, he accumulated fifteen others of various sizes. The smallest of those he was to destroy for the sake of psychic science weighed fifteen pounds, the largest tipped the scales at seventy. He did not specify the breeds, but he did write that the scales "were sensitive to one-sixteenth of an ounce."

Killing the animals on the scales with drugs in order "to secure the quiet and freedom necessary to keep the beam at balance," Dr. MacDougall discovered a weight loss in every test. Not at the moment of death, but approximately twenty or thirty minutes later. This occurred, he explained, when the urine expelled at death evaporated. A similar quantity of water on the scales evaporated in precisely the same amount of time.

Dr. MacDougall concluded that men and dogs were not the same physiologically—that men have souls, while dogs, and probably other animals, do not.

Even before the public at large learned about Dr. MacDougall's experiments, when many outraged citizens were to condemn him for his callous treatment of dying humans and his cruelty to animals, Hereward Carrington, a member of the American Society for Psychical Research's editorial staff, took him to task in the same *Journal* in which his article appeared—and for another reason.

Perhaps because Carrington was unusually thin and could not gain weight by eating fatty foods, he had studied nutritional, as well as psychic phenomena. He had learned that one woman, after fasting four days, had added eight pounds by eating merely a shallow portion of soup and three light meals. Another grew heavier, not lighter, in the course of an eight-day fast. A man named Estrapper went without food for a week, prior to an athletic event at Madison Square Garden, and as a result weighed three-quarters of a pound more than he had before.

Unexplained weight losses could be just as perplexing. One dieter who fasted three days, then ate on the fourth, shed forty pounds in twenty-one days. Another, at the end of a three-week fasting regime, lost seventy-five pounds. These women, Carrington noted, had been unusually heavy, but there were people troubled by mental problems who, though they ate normally, lost more poundage than they would have on a strict reducing diet.

Carrington cited another remarkable case, reported by Rear Admiral George W. Melville to the Smithsonian Institution in Washington. A man, enclosed in an airtight metal coffin for an hour in a town in New England, was five pounds lighter after his ordeal.

Dr. MacDougall replied to Carrington's criticism by pointing out that his listing of weight losses did not explain why they happened. As to the man confined in the casket, it was likely that he had perspired away the missing five pounds.

The president of the American Society for Psychical Research, Dr. James H. Hyslop, had his say on the matter, observing "that the problem of psychic research is not affected by either success or failure in such experiments as Dr. MacDougall's. . . . Proving the loss of weight by death in some way not ordinarily accountable by physical theories would not prove that the residuum was a soul. It might be some vital energy, and the soul yet remain an imponderable form of substance."

There was no rush to replicate Dr. MacDougall's soul-weighing tests. More than thirty years passed before another series of similar experiments was made, this time in California. H. L. Twining, the author of *The Physical Theory of the Soul* (1915) conducted his research with mice. In one experiment a live mouse had been dropped into a test tube, then held in place by wads of cotton forced in around and above it. The open end of the tube was sealed by the flame of a Bunsen burner. The tube containing the mouse was put on one tray of the experimenter's scales; a matching tube and weights rested on the other. The trays were balanced before the rodent suffocated. There was no loss of weight, either at the moment the mouse died or afterward. The tubes and the equipment were kept in place over night; the trays were still balanced in the morning. If a substance had separated from the mouse, it must have been retained in the sealed tube, Twining wrote.

After another mouse had been inserted in a flask, and the open end closed with a rubber stopper, this flask and another one, plus weights, were balanced on the scales. At first, to the surprise of the experimenter, the mouse, which could be seen through the transparent enclosure, did not suffocate. But when the porous stopper had been covered with paraffin, the mouse soon ceased breathing. Again the balance of the trays was not disturbed.

Twining also put a mouse into a glass container with an open top. He was amazed that the mouse succumbed in a far shorter time than he had expected. As he explained it, carbon dioxide produced by the rodent's respiration accumulated at the bottom of the container. Oxygen, lighter in weight, could not descend from the air outside and circulate in the enclosure.

A weight loss had been noted in this test. Twining thought that perhaps the perspiration generated by the carbon dioxide poisoning had vaporized and forced the carbon dioxide out of the container. Testing this assumption, Twining placed two flasks, each containing the same amount of water, on the trays. He submerged a mouse in one flask and added weights equivalent to the mouse's body on the other tray. The trays remained perfectly balanced after the mouse drowned.

Not having exhausted his supply of mice, the researcher dropped one into a flask that had been filled in part with calcium chloride. The mouth of the flask was sealed with a stopper, from which glass tubes protruded at the top and bottom. Any vaporized moisture emanating from the mouse would have to pass through the chemical to leave the flask. Another flask and sufficient weights to balance the first rested on the second tray. As in the previous test, no loss of weight occurred when the mouse died. The calcium chloride absorbed the moisture.

Twining wrote that after some thirty different tests, which were repeated, he had found no unexplained losses of weight after death. Twining confirmed the validity of his tests in a letter written to Hereward Carrington on September 13, 1933.

In most research procedures preliminary experiments are made with rodents or other small animals before the tests are tried with humans. The reverse took place during the soul-weighing studies. Though no humans were slaughtered, fifteen dogs and many mice were destroyed in the attempts to provide proof of man's spirituality.

5.

The Shape
of the Soul

In 1921, at the First International Psychical Congress
in Copenhagen, Hereward Carrington, the first man to devote
his life to psychical research in the United States, proposed
a scientific experiment designed to reveal the shape of a soul.
At the age of forty Carrington had earned a worldwide reputa-
tion as an authority through his investigations of many phases
of paranormal phenomena and his many articles and books
on the subject. Skeptical, yet asserting that a few people had
authentic psychic ability and that there were many areas to
explore, he appealed to both doubters and believers.

The soul-shape experiment that he described in Denmark
was one of many that Carrington hoped to try in a scientific
laboratory—if he could find wealthy sponsors. An airtight
aluminum box was to be suspended inside a hermetically
sealed container. The subject of the test—a cat, dog, or a
monkey—could be observed through a window in the inner
box and the glass sides of the larger enclosure. The space
between the boxes was to have "an atmosphere of perfectly
dust-free air or water vapor" like that in the Cloud Chamber
devised by C. T. R. Wilson, a physicist, for his studies of
ionized alpha and beta rays.

After the animal had been killed by gas piped into the

aluminum box, some of the air was to be pumped out quickly. The rapid expansion of the remaining air would instantly lower the temperature, causing the vapor "to condense upon the ions" of the animal's soul, which, according to Carrington's hypothesis, would be trapped behind the transparent panels of the outer container. "Therefore," he explained, "when condensation occurs, the resulting line will outline the form of the astral body." If the animal had a soul, and if the soul was detached and ionized, an experimenter would be able to see and photograph it before the shape dissolved.

The American delegate's proposal had been applauded by his colleagues in Europe; but his theory was not put to the test until more than a decade later. Then Dr. R. A. Watters, physicist and project planner for the Dr. William Bernard Johnston Foundation for Biophysical Research of Reno, Nevada, wrote Carrington for more detailed information, enclosing an article that he had written on "Biological Sources of Radio Activity" in the May 1931 issue of the *Archives of Physical Therapy.* Carrington sent a comprehensive and encouraging reply.

The Cloud Chamber that Dr. Watters constructed was not as large as Carrington had visualized. The experiments were to be made with grasshoppers, frogs, mice, and chicks. Some of the subjects did not die when they were gassed; others withstood jolts of electricity. Finally, a small guillotine was installed in the Cloud Chamber. When its sharp blade fell, death was inevitable.

Despite these technical problems, the first series of experiments produced positive results. Cloudy mists with dark areas suggesting astral masses appeared in fourteen of the fifty photographs taken in the laboratory. Dr. Watters's pamphlet *The Intra-atomic Quality* emphasized that the murky material manifested only after an animal died, not when it survived either the gas or electric-shock ordeals.

Affirmative soul experiments were so rarely published that B. J. Hopper, a British investigator, ran a similar series of tests for Dr. Nandor Fodor's International Institute for Psychical Research in London. The results were completely negative. Hopper's *Enquiry into the Cloud-Chamber Method of Studying the "Intra-atomic Quality"* (1936) charged that the American psychist's laboratory tests must have been carelessly conducted.

Dr. Watters replied that the techniques used in the tests by his critic were not precisely the same as those he had used himself. Spurred on by Hopper's barbs, Dr. Watters designed and operated an intricate Cloud Chamber which, Carrington said, was as much an improvement over the one he had specified originally as a page printed by the latest, most up-to-date presses compared to one pulled from manually assembled type.

There was no doubt that misty material really arose after an animal died; there was a question as to the chemical composition of this material. With the improved apparatus the American physicist eventually found that, contrary to his initial supposition, intra-atomic emanations had not been the source of the phenomena. Following an animal's death, the chemistry of decay generated the cloudy masses. This was the natural result of decomposition, not evidence that a soul had been liberated.

Cloud Chamber Investigations into Post-Mortem Ions (1939), an illustrated bulletin prepared by Dr. Watters and his mentor Dr. Johnston, told how the flaws of the early experiments had been corrected and described how the apparatus then being used could be built.

Assessing the outcome of the Cloud-Chamber controversy in *The Invisible World* (1946), Carrington, reluctant to admit that the soul-shape experiment he had proposed a quarter of a century earlier had been a fiasco, wrote that there were still phases of it to be pondered. Why, for example, did the cloud hovering above the body of a dead mouse in one of Dr. Watters's photographs look like a mouse and not like a grasshopper or a frog? Carrington asked this question, but did not answer it.

Carrington was then sixty-five. Though he had written more on the subject than any of his contemporaries, had

had séances with many famous mediums, and had tried to validate survival theories and the experiments of European and American investigators, he frankly admitted that he had not found a shred of evidence that would convince skeptical scientists.

Born Hereward Hubert Lavington Carrington of British parents in December 1880 on Jersey, an English Channel Island, he had been brought to Minneapolis, Minnesota, at the age of eight. Ten years later, while scanning the shelves of an antiquarian bookshop for volumes on the lore of leger-demain, his hobby, he had seen, purchased, and been enth-ralled by *Essays in Psychical Research* (1899) by Miss X (Ada Goodrich Freer), a member of the Society for Psychical Re-search. The following year, after reading the society's *Proceedings,* he joined the American branch of the English organization.

The letters he received from Dr. Richard Hodgson, secre-tary of the American section in Boston, as well as Dr. Hodg-son's masterfully presented investigative reports in the socie-ty's publications, inspired Carrington. This, he decided, was a man worthy of emulation.

Carrington had moved to New York and was working as an assistant to Dr. James H. Hyslop, former Columbia Univer-sity professor of logic and ethics, when his idol died and the Boston office of the English society closed. Carrington aided Dr. Hyslop in the organization of the present American Society for Psychical Research, established in 1907.

The fledgling investigator journeyed to Windsor, Nova Scotia, in January 1907 on his first assignment—a poltergeist case. A judge of the Probate Court there had written that objects, hurled by an unseen force, had crashed in shops and on the streets. Light bulbs shattered mysteriously, eggs cracked while on display in crates, money dropped from the air.

The morning after Carrington's arrival, he went with the judge to a store on the principal street. Minutes later, an apple flew by their heads and landed on the floor. A heavy iron spike fell from above as the men entered a furniture factory. While they were on the first floor, coins clattered down, a barrel began rolling in their direction, and a stack of rattan chairs tilted, teetered, and then toppled over.

On the second floor of the plant several chairs, standing side by side in a row, started to rock simultaneously. "I actually saw them *start* in their movement, and the movement of the chairs increase in violence while I was looking at them," Carrington noted. Wishing to get a closer view of the backs of the rockers, he crawled under and around an accumulation of clutter. Not visible from the front was a piece of string. One end had been tied in place. The other passed over the backs of the rockers, then down and out of sight through a hole. By tugging the string, someone on the floor below could activate the chairs.

Carrington did not tell the judge about this discovery. The judge was talking with a disembodied voice. He believed that spirits of the dead could communicate and expressed no surprise when the low, muffled voice of an unseen presence addressed him. While he questioned the phantom from the afterlife, Carrington tried to locate the source of the sound. One end of a long rubber hose had been concealed in a heap of furniture. The other end of the flexible speaking tube, like the string attached to the chairs, ran through an opening in the floor to a talker on the street level of the factory.

A moment before a stack of chairs wobbled and fell, Carrington saw the hand of a worker give the stack a quick shove. Instead of identifying the culprit, Carrington echoed the judge's words of amazement. The workers continued their well-planned harassment. One would speak to attract the judge's attention, while another, behind him, threw an object over his head, then put his hands in his pockets before the judge could turn around. Later that afternoon, after talking with merchants on the main street, Carrington realized that almost the entire town had conspired to taunt the judge.

The story of this plot appeared in the first volume of the *Proceedings* of the new American Society for Psychical Research. The Windsor judge read the article, but refused to believe it. "When a man has reached this stage of credulity," Carrington commented later, "it is, of course, useless to argue with him further."

A two-week stay at Lily Dale, a summer camp for spiritualists in upstate New York, also disappointed the seeker of authentic phenomena. His knowledge of the psychology of deception, acquired as an amateur conjurer, enabled him to detect the tricks of every spirit photographer, producer of messages on slates, and specialist in materializations that he observed. His devastating report on Lily Dale in the second volume of the *Proceedings of the American Society for Psychical Research* and his extensive revelation of the ruses of fraudulent mediums in his 426-page *The Physical Phenomena of Spiritualism* (1907) served as a guide for other investigators who were not as experienced or disillusioned as himself.

While visiting the headquarters of the Society for Psychical Research in London in November 1908, Carrington was invited to be part of a team going to Naples the following month for test settings with the most famous and controversial medium in Europe, Eusapia Palladino.

At the end of the second séance with the short, plump, tempestuous Neapolitan, the Honorable Everard Feilding, an experienced British investigator, and the American expert on mediumistic deceit were so bewildered that they wired London for reinforcements. W. W. Baggally, a member of the Council of the English society and, like Carrington, an amateur magician, arrived in time for the fifth séance. After the eleventh and final sitting the opinion of the testers was unanimous. They had observed supernormal phenomena!

A table had been levitated from the floor, strange forms had materialized, and objects had moved, apparently on their own volition, Carrington wrote in his portion of the report published in Volume twenty-three of the British *Proceedings*. He had been "forced to the conclusion that these phenomena were genuine," when something touched him—he didn't know what it was—as Eusapia's hands and feet were held by a colleague and himself.

The Italian woman's phenomena were the only authentic physical manifestations that he had ever encountered, Carrington proclaimed in *Eusapia Palladino and Her Phenomena* (1909). That November the fifty-four-year-old medium arrived in New York to give a series of séances under Carrington's management. These were not for qualified scientific investigators to test her psychic abilities, but for anyone who would pay a high fee to observe her in action.

Dr. Hyslop, of the American Society for Psychical Research, was not invited. Dr. Saram R. Ellison, a founder of the Society of American Magicians and an old friend of Carrington's, attended the second performance. His verdict: "By substitution of hands and feet she could have done any of the manifestations." That is, by releasing a hand or a foot when both were apparently held, she could amaze her patrons. Professor Hugo Münsterberg, a Harvard psychologist, was even more to the point in his article in the February 1910 issue of *Metropolitan Magazine*. He wrote that a sitter (Edgar Scott) had slipped from his chair in the dimly lighted séance room and sprawled on the floor behind and to the left of the medium. When a stool moved noisily, he reached out to make sure that a string was not attached to it and grabbed the motivating force—Eusapia's foot. She had freed it, though those sitting adjacent to her had thought both feet were under control.

The most damaging of many exposures was written by a psychologist, Dr. Joseph Jastrow, for the May 4, 1910, issue of *Collier's Weekly*. Joseph F. Rinn and Warner C. Pyne, clad in black coveralls, had crawled into the dining room of Columbia professor Herbert G. Lord's house while a Palladino séance was in progress. Positioning themselves under the table, they saw the medium's foot strike a table leg to produce raps. As the table tilted to the right, due to pressure of her right hand on the surface, they saw her put her left foot under the left table leg. Pressing down on the tabletop with her left hand and up with her left foot under the table leg to form a clamp, she lifted her foot and "levitated" the table from the floor.

Ridiculed by feature writers, censured by editorials, and

caricatured by cartoonists, Palladino sailed for Italy. The Honorable Everard Feilding returned to Naples to verify his own earlier enthusiastic endorsement of Eusapia's supernormal phenomena. With him this time was William Marriott, a magician knowledgeable in the methods of mediums. Nothing occurred at the Palladino séances that could not be explained. Her marvelous powers seemed to have evaporated.

Carrington's credibility as an impartial commentator on the psychic scene suffered a staggering blow after the exposures in New York, but he continued to maintain that at least some of Eusapia's phenomena were authentic. Conscious that the public was in no mood for tales of miracles, he appeared at the Berkeley Theater in September 1910 with an exposure of fraudulent marvels. Among other feats he demonstrated and explained "The Rapping Hand" and "The Spirit Bell." For a finale he produced a luminous ghost from a curtained cabinet.

Had he denounced Palladino as a complete fraud, Carrington's competence as an investigator would have been challenged. That he was a perceptive observer is shown by many of his laboratory experiments and his astute assessments of perplexing issues. As an accepted authority, writer of popular books, and lecturer, he knew that far more people were interested in mysteries than explanations. He capitalized on the mood of the moment but did not censure all alleged psychic phenomena. Unless there is something to investigate, there is no need for a psychical researcher. If Carrington was less than fully honest in his public statements, it may have been because he realized that without the support of believers in supernormal marvels, he would not be able to pursue his chosen career.

Lecturing for the Brooklyn Philosophical Association on "Does Psychical Research Evidence Warrant Belief in a Spirit World," Carrington declared, early in January 1913, that "there was something in spiritualism, but it would require at least two hundred years to solve the problem." "Most of the audience didn't have that long to wait," wrote the *Telegraph* reporter who covered the event, "since they were expected home for a 6 o'clock dinner." He added that "Mr. Carrington talked learnedly without saying anything."

The Brooklyn *Standard Union* reported that Palladino's former manager "confessed she was a fraud, and is now living in Italy, having lost her powers as a result of her exposures . . . he also admitted that ninety-eight percent of so-called mediumistic phenomena is fraudulent, the remaining two percent forming a basis for genuine psychic research."

Carrington cited the cold breeze that sometimes came from a scar on Eusapia's head as one of the manifestations that convinced him of her unusual powers. He did not think that this cold current was merely air. "It was a psychic agitation of the ether, . . . the externalized vital energy in the medium."

Edward Dobson, an ex-president of the Philosophical Association, replied that the most important evidence presented by the speaker to validate psychic phenomena—the alleged wind from a scar—"was enough to blow up his whole case." This would be rejected in any court as "immaterial, irrelevant and incompetent." The New York *Sun* commented that Carrington's loyalty to the medium he had managed was "extremely moving," but if the many exposures of Palladino were of no import, there was no reason to discuss "such a novel hypothesis as 'psychical agitation of the ether.' "

Eusapia died in Naples in 1918. Four years later her name was linked with Carrington's again. He had organized his own research group in New York—the American Psychical Institute. Sir Arthur Conan Doyle, then lecturing on spiritualism in the United States, came with his wife to a séance arranged by the two-year-old organization. The medium Nino Pecorara, a young Italian, after having been bound at the wrists and ankles with piano wire by Carrington, sat behind closed drapes in an alcove of the room. According to the April 19, 1922, issue of the New York *World,* moans, snorts, and whispers were heard from the alcove. The curtain bulged forward. The Doyles felt a cold breeze. A shriek preceeded the toss of a tambourine through an opening in the curtain. An unseen bell rang; notes were played on a toy piano on the far side of the drapes; a little table came forward, then toppled over.

A voice announced, "I who used to call the spirits back, now come back to be a spirit myself."

Carrington asked, "Is that you, Madame Palladino?"

"Yes," was the whispered reply.

"The power is getting stronger," Sir Arthur commented. "We send you our love and our best encouragement."

"We are glad to meet you again," the medium's former manager broke in. "You used to produce wonderful phenomena and I hope you will try to help us tonight."

While Pecorara flabbergasted the believers that night, he did not do nearly so well the following winter when he applied for one of the two $2,500 prizes offered by *Scientific American* to mediums who could produce phenomena under test conditions. Psychologist William McDougall; physicist Daniel F. Comstock; Walter Franklin Prince, research officer of the American Society for Psychical Research; Houdini, the magician; and Hereward Carrington had been named as members of the supervising committee. When Houdini, a specialist in escapes, bound Pecorara to a chair, no phenomena were produced.

The outstanding contender was "Margery" (Mina Crandon), the vivacious young wife of a prominent Boston surgeon. She had been credited with a wide range of manifestations—cool breezes, tilting tables, floating trumpets, bell ringing, and messages from the dead.

Committee member Carrington lived at the Crandon house on Lime Street while he investigated the medium. In later years he confessed to friends that he had had an affair with Margery during this period. He stressed that this did not influence his judgment on the case. Houdini and Walter Franklin Prince thought otherwise.

When, finally, in February 1925 the *Scientific American* committee's verdict on Margery was announced, it was learned that she had been denied the prize by a vote of four to one. Only Carrington insisted that some of her phenomena had been authentic, a phrase he had used earlier after the Palladino exposures in New York.

Taking advantage of the publicity he had received as a member of the *Scientific American* committee, Carrington presented "The Spirit World—Marvelous Demonstrations of Psychic Phenomena" for the week beginning August 17, 1925, in the grand ballroom of the Astor Hotel on Broadway. Among the attractions were Khaldah, a mentalist; Leona LaMar, a vaudeville clairvoyant; and Philip Voros, "The Psychical Healer and Master of Thought-Transference." Carrington introduced the acts and ran a film, *Fraudulent Mediums Unmasked*, revealing how tables could be lifted, messages conjured up on slates, and ghosts materialized with the aid of luminous cheesecloth. A reporter for the *Herald Tribune* wrote than an "enthusiastic audience laughed and gasped" during the first performance.

Readers of Carrington's books receive the impression that he "investigated" the feats of fakirism presented by Rahman Bey and, later, Hamid Bey. Actually, he toured with them in vaudeville, telling the public that their stunts of pain resistance and living burial were authentic demonstrations of supernormal power, which they were not. I first saw Carrington when, as a boy in Baltimore, I watched while he supervised the onstage burial of Hamid Bey. He also lectured in American and Canadian vaudeville theaters for Labero, a European hypnotist who performed with chickens, snakes, and crocodiles.

For a time Carrington managed Bert Reese, an expert switcher of folded slips of paper, who convinced Thomas Alva Edison that mental power, not manipulation and showmanship, enabled him to read the inventor's thoughts. Princess Serene, another "clairvoyant," also traveled under Carrington's sponsorship.

Between these activities and lecture engagements, Carrington found time to revive his dormant American Psychical Institute for a few years. Joseph Mitchell, a New York *World-Telegram* feature writer, reported in April 1934 that the "vegetarian, magician, agnostic, and director of the American Psy-

chical Institute, who has been hunting ghosts and astral bodies for thirty-five years much as other men hunt dollar bills
or moose" had completed tests with an English medium that
seemed "to demonstrate the survival of disembodied spirits."
The medium was Mrs. Eileen Garrett. Carrington told the
reporter that "the alleged spirit on the other side who controls her is called Uvani, an Arab who says he lived about
100 years ago. He talks through Mrs. Garrett whenever she
goes into a trance." The money that financed the tests came
from Dr. Adolph Meyer, director of the Henry Phipps Psychiatric Clinic at Johns Hopkins Hospital in Baltimore, and was
part of an "intuition fund." There were nine monitored
séances with the medium in 1932 and fifteen more in 1933.

After Mrs. Garrett's hands were taped to the terminals
of a lie detector—a galvanometer—and before she became
entranced, a standard hundred-word psychological association test began. After each word was read, she called out
another word suggested by it. The word "hunger" brought
the response "thirst." A phrase came when "sleep" was mentioned—"it's nice."

Entering a trance and speaking as Uvani, she responded
to "sleep" with "peace," while "hunger" triggered "sad-
ness." A stopwatch timed the intervals between test words
and replies. The Uvani answers were completely different
from the ones uttered by the medium in a normal condition.

Through the spirit control, Uvani, other spirits took the
word association test. These responses were rarely the same
as the ones given by Uvani or Mrs. Garrett. Studying ten
thousand reactions to the hundred key words, Carrington
found that on only four occasions were the medium's responses precisely the same as the spirits'. He maintained that
this experiment was "the nearest approach so far to scientific
proof of life after death."

Asked how Uvani, the Arab who had lived so long ago,
had acquired his knowledge of English, the psychical researcher replied, "We asked him that and he said that he
impresses his thoughts on Mrs. Garrett's mind and they are

translated by her." Carrington rejected the idea that the spirits were indicative of a split personality. "Personalities split off through natural psychiatric disturbances always have a recognizable leakage from one to another."

Years later, when Eileen Garrett became a publisher, she issued Carrington's account of the word-association tests, *The Case for Psychic Survival* (1957), and another book for which he had not found an outlet, *The American Seances with Eusapia Palladino* (1954).

In the summer of 1941 Carrington's voice reached a larger audience than ever before on a Saturday-night radio program, "Who Knows?" The show, originating in the New York studio of WOR, dramatized eerie psychic stories from his files. Carrington was then living in a Greenwich Village brownstone. He told a reporter from the *New York Times* that though he had no psychic powers himself, he had had experiences he could not explain. After the death of a woman he had known, a brass knocker on his door rapped several times. When he opened the door, no one was there. A note also sounded on his piano, though neither he nor anyone else was near the instrument. Once, he recalled, he entered a room in an alleged haunted house in Westchester and received "an astral wallop in the stomach." He was told later that a woman had strangled herself with a noose in the room.

Professional actors played the roles of mediums on Carrington's radio programs. Psychics were unreliable. After Amelia Earhart, the first woman to make a successful flight across the Atlantic Ocean, disappeared somewhere over the Pacific, Carrington asked Eileen Garrett to go into a trance and try to reach her. A recording was to be made of the séance; then the electrical transcription was to be broadcast. At the séance the voice of Uvani, her spirit guide, issued from Mrs. Garrett's lips, saying, "If my medium has no more respect for me than to try this silly experiment, I'm going to part company with her."

Mrs. Garrett had been annoyed when she opened her eyes

and was informed of this declaration. According to Carrington, "She wanted the chance to appear on the radio very badly."

Carrington moved to Hollywood before his book *The Invisible World* was published in 1946. He still hoped for stronger proof that personality survives death than that he had obtained through the word-association tests with Mrs. Garrett. Tall and thin, with his white hair combed up and back from a high forehead, he had a professorial appearance and engaging manner that delighted those who attended his public lectures and his private psychic-study classes in his studio-apartment on Vine Street.

In *The Invisible World* he offered himself "as a sort of psychic guinea pig" for several experiments that could be made at the time of his death. A physician on the staff of St. Thomas's Hospital in London had used dicyanin, a substance made from coal tar, to enhance his ability to see the auras of living people. Dr. Walter J. Kilner claimed that the luminous radiations grew fainter as a patient died. Carrington thought that a test to prove or disprove this statement should be tried.

Another worthwhile experiment, previously conducted only with animals, had been described by Dr. Elmer Gates in the June 1906 issue of the *Annals of Psychical Science*. "When the body is alive," Dr. Gates wrote, "it is a bundle of electric currents, and electric waves cannot pass through these currents; but when they cease, at death, the body becomes transparent to electric waves."

Carrington noted that an instrument called a lastrometer had been installed in some séance rooms in attempts to measure the amount of energy accumulated. Possibly, he wrote, the apparatus could detect the energy surging from a dying body. If, as investigators in France had concluded, soul substances caused screens of calcium sulphide to glow brilliantly, this spectacular display should also be arranged.

There were other experiments with ultraviolet and infrared rays that appealed to the veteran researcher, but the one that intrigued him most was a larger version of the Cloud Chamber test he had suggested at the First International

Psychical Congress in Denmark. If, he wrote, further experimentation produced more affirmative results and if a man-size Cloud Chamber could be constructed, he would volunteer as a subject.

Carrington seldom mentioned these after-death experiments to his friends. He preferred to talk about Dr. J. B. Rhine's ESP studies at Duke University, a new trick he had seen at a magic shop, or his interest in nutrition. (Once he had lived for two years solely on raw fruit and nuts.)

He died on December 26, 1958, at the age of seventy-eight. No provisions had been made for any of the experiments that he had listed in print thirteen years earlier. The super Cloud Chamber was never built. The shape of a soul is still a matter of conjecture.

6.

Dimensions of
the Soul

Hereward Carrington's proposed soul-shape experiment had not been a success when tested by other researchers. He had not tried it himself during the years when he had had his own laboratory, but he did attempt to replicate soul experiments that had been made in Europe. The most unusual of these had been designed by a Dutch physicist, Dr. J. L. W. P. Matla, who believed that messages sent from the dead were carried by an invisible substance called by some a soul or a spirit. He preferred to term the mysterious material a man-force.

Dr. Matla had experimented in The Hague with compressed air and high-frequency electricity. These unseen but powerful forces could be detected with sensitive instruments. It seemed logical to him that the man-force could be isolated and measured. In the spring of 1904 he supervised the construction of a special chamber for his research. Approximately six feet wide, seven feet long, and nine feet high, it had a thick concrete floor, which he was sure would minimize the effect of possible outside disturbances, such as vibrations from other parts of the building or subterranean tremors.

There was a shielded glass window in the door that led to the experimental area from the adjacent corridor. When the blind was open, Dr. Matla and other observers could monitor the tests by peering through the glass. Traditionally, séance rooms are darkened for physical manifestations and materializations. Though heavy dark curtains covered the walls of Dr. Matla's small laboratory, the flames of acetylene torches illuminated the interior.

The apparatus that Dr. Matla installed in the chamber would have perplexed any scientist who tried to guess its purpose. The principal piece was an empty cardboard cylinder, approximately twenty inches tall and ten inches wide. One end of a small rubber hose had been fitted into a hole near the top. Then the cylinder had been wrapped in tinfoil and hermetically sealed. The other end of the hose was securely fastened to a measuring device that Dr. Matla dubbed a manometer.

Theoretically, if any portion of the man-force penetrated the sealed cylinder, the displaced air would be forced through the hose to the manometer, where the pressure would motivate the single drop of alcohol in a horizontal glass tube. Calibrations on the glass would then indicate how much air had been displaced. When this was known, it would be a simple matter to calculate the amount of space occupied by the imperceptible presence.

How, you may wonder, did Dr. Matla summon the man-force and persuade it to seep into the sealed cylinder? According to the experimenter himself and his associate, Dr. G. L. Zaalberg van Zelst, he politely requested the invisible matter to follow his instructions. As the man-force did not reply and could not be seen, the only way that observers could tell whether it was cooperating was to look through the window and watch the drop of alcohol in the manometer. The details of the experiments are given in *Het geheim van den dood,* published in The Hague in 1911 and in a French translation, *Le mystère de la mort,* issued in Paris the following year.

Apparently as soon as the man-force understood the part it was to play, the movement of the alcohol in the glass tube indicated that air was being displaced in the sealed cylinder.

Discovering that the cylinder, which could hold twenty-two liters, was not large enough to accommodate the entire man-force, Dr. Matla constructed another one almost twice as large. This also proved too small, as did a cylinder with a fifty-liter capacity. He progressed to containers more capacious, fifty-five and sixty liters, and eventually found that the man-force occupied a space equivalent to about fifty-three liters. It was difficult to establish the precise amount because the force could expand an additional 1.26 mm or contract approximately 8 mm.

To insure that the man-force, and not some other influence, was causing the fluctuations of his measuring instrument, the experimenter placed another sealed cylinder, attached to a second manometer, along with the first in the isolated chamber. When only the first indicated the force's presence, he ruled out the disturbing possibility that atmospheric conditions had produced the astonishing results.

An ocean away, Dr. Duncan MacDougall had observed during his research with dying patients that the first soul to be weighed had tipped the scales three-quarters of an ounce. Dr. Matla, who was not aware of the study being made in Massachusetts, found the man-force to be heavier in Holland—about two and a quarter ounces. He calculated that the specific weight was approximately 12.24 mg less than hydrogen and more than 176 times lighter than air. He also noted that it was unwise to suggest that the man-force elevate itself beyond a certain point, as it would disintegrate.

Dr. Matla stressed that a medium had not been present during the years that he studied the man-force. Some people who read his book suggested that the physicist was himself a medium. How else could he have succeeded in getting the man-force to manifest, or have received a hint from it that he should invent an elaborate machine through which it could communicate with him? This machine, the "dynamistograph" that Dr. Matla made next, was as complex as his cylinder had been simple. Mounted on the top of a table was a stand that supported an upright disk, similar in appearance to a clockface except that letters of the alphabet replaced numerals. A motor turned the disk slowly.

A slight pressure on an intricate braking system, which rested on a large platform by the table, would stop the revolving disk. The letter at the bottom of the dial would then be imprinted on a roll of paper tape by a lever striking an inked ribbon. In essence, the dynamistograph was a typewriter operated by pressure on a single key. As each letter was imprinted, the paper tape unrolled one space. The messages were read from the top of the tape to the bottom, rather than across a page.

For twelve months the obliging man-force typed out messages—even when the experimenters were not in the building. Sometimes the words made sense, sometimes not. The man-force performed best in warm weather and became erratic when the temperature fell.

Hereward Carrington had been impressed by the arduous researches of the Dutch physicist. For many years, in his books and lectures, he had crusaded for the creation of a richly endowed American laboratory where important psychic issues could be studied and perhaps resolved. The Institut Général Psychologique in Paris received substantial support from government sources for similar studies, Carrington maintained. Several organizations in Italy had quarters where experiments and investigations were made.

The Society for Psychical Research in London had a number of research officers and sufficient money to operate successfully. There were efficient groups in Russia, Germany, Switzerland, and Portugal. Now that the great Boston investigators, Professor William James and Dr. Richard Hodgson, had died, only Professor James H. Hyslop, of the American Society for Psychical Research, and Carrington himself were prominent in the field in the United States.

Carrington yearned to become even more prominent. His *Modern Psychical Phenomena* (1919) contained a lengthy and sympathetic account of Dr. Matla's activities in Holland. A year later Carrington founded the American Psychical Institute in New York City. It closed down in 1922, but he revived it ten years later and began to conduct the sort of laboratory experiments that he had only written about in the past.

Dr. Matla's man-force experiments had fascinated him. He decided that he would try to replicate them, something, he said, that no other investigator had attempted to do. Several members of his organization were invited to serve as observers during the tests. They gathered in New York one warm afternoon. A thermometer in the room where a sealed cylinder and a manometer had been placed rose to seventy-eight degrees Fahrenheit.

As there was no window in the door to the room, a ringing device had been attached to the manometer. Movement of a drop of alcohol would close an electrical circuit and cause a bell to clang. Carrington and his friends sat in the adjoining room. He asked "any force present, capable of entering the cylinder and displacing the air, please to do so."

No sound came from behind the closed door. He repeated the request. Again there was silence. He opened the door and walked over to the manometer. The drop of alcohol was gone! Not far, however. It had dropped out of view into the bulb of the measuring instrument. After inserting another drop in the glass tube, Carrington returned to the adjacent room.

When he again called for the force, following a short delay, the bell sounded briefly, then stopped. Some of the alcohol, he found, had adhered to the electrodes that triggered the sound system. When a third drop was inserted in the glass tube and the force invoked, the bell rang steadily for seventy-five seconds.

This experiment, Carrington said, demonstrated that the manometer had not been assembled properly, that he had tinkered too much with the alcohol, and that capillary action—not the presence of the force in the cylinder—might have closed the circuit and started the bell ringing.

After the manometer had been repaired, three more experiments were conducted. During the second, the bell sounded a bit less than two minutes after the force had been spoken to. The bell did not ring in the third test until Carrington entered the room with the equipment.

The bell was silent throughout the fourth experiment, though when Carrington approached the measuring instrument, the alcohol oscillated. A powerful magnet hanging above the sealed cylinder in the fifth experiment did not attract the man-force or have a measurable effect on the manometer. The sixth experiment centered on the measuring device to determine whether it would give a reading without the man-force being called.

Dr. Matla had conducted many different tests in The Hague, so did the American experimenter in New York. When the sealed cylinder was suspended from one of a pair of balances and the other weighted to keep the two aligned, there was no evidence that the man-force entered the cylinder. The scales did not tip and the bell, which would have been activated by this movement, did not ring.

Many of the experiments were made in a lighted chamber, others in a dark room. The latter involved two sealed cylinders, scales, a light projector, and a screen in the adjacent chamber. An ionization device and an electroscope were employed in an effort to detect ionization after the force entered the cylinder.

At the end of more than a year of experimentation, Carrington reported in an American Psychical Institute *Bulletin* that changes of temperature and also coincidence caused the phenomena that the Dutch physicist had attributed to the man-force. Carrington had discovered that when the temperature fell, the alcohol would recede; when the temperature rose, the alcohol would advance. Slight variances of climate caused the phenomena, he concluded, not an invisible power termed a man-force.

Steam heat in winter and hot weather in summer generated warm air currents that activated the drop of alcohol in the measuring instrument. Further, the body heat of an observer approaching the manometer frequently made the alcohol quiver and move.

To verify the validity of his man-force theory, Dr. Matla

had placed two identical sealed cylinders and manometers side by side in his laboratory. Only the first manometer had responded when the force had been asked to enter the cylinder to which it was attached.

Carrington's tests with a pair of cylinders and manometers had contradictory results. When the cylinders were together, the one not designated for the force produced the same reading on its measuring device as the other. When the cylinders were widely separated, the readings varied. This happened, Carrington found, because the air surrounding the equipment was not at a constant temperature in different areas of the room.

Having solved the problem of the cylinders with a natural explanation, Carrington turned his attention to Dr. Matla's dynamistograph, the machine through which the dead allegedly communicated with the living. Rather than build a complete replica of the complicated typing system, Carrington started at the beginning, with the key that stopped the turning letter-disk and motivated the printing action. Dr. Matla had claimed that the pressure of an unseen force on the key controlled the action of the machine. Could an invisible something exert the required pressure? What was this mysterious something? These were the questions that the experimenter in New York hoped to answer.

The stopping and starting key built by Carrington was a membrane-covered tube. Minimal pressure on the membrane closed an electrical circuit and rang a bell. As long as pressure was maintained, the bell rang. Had the connecting wires extended to a motor-driven disk and a printing system, printed communications could have been received. The far simpler bell hookup permitted the experimenter to receive messages with less preparation. If the letters of the alphabet were recited slowly and the bell sounded after the letters *n* and *o*, the answer to a question posed earlier was unmistakably no.

Mechanically, the Carrington device worked too well. If a door was opened a room away, if Carrington put a book on a table or opened a pack of cigarettes, the bell rang. The slightest vibration affected it. When he replaced the membrane with less sensitive material, the "phenomena" ceased.

Two of Carrington's friends constructed another variation of Dr. Matla's machine. Aluminum plates, arranged so that the surfaces would not touch, were installed in a case, with the lower edges of the vertical plates resting on insulating material; the upper sections of the plates were insulated by the atmosphere around them. The plates were alternately attached to terminals that extended from the housing. A connection was formed consisting of one terminal, a galvanometer, a switch, several batteries, and the earth. Another series of links was made between the other terminal, the earth, and the case.

After the switch had been thrown, the investigators knew by the movement of the galvanometer needle that the circuit had closed. As they believed in communication with the dead, they had no hesitancy in talking to an unseen force. They asked whether it could move the needle; the needle quivered. They accepted this as a sign that the force had understood the question and responded. They asked the force to move the needle again; the needle vibrated. They suggested that the force withdraw; the needle became motionless.

Instructing the force to influence the needle if the answer to a question was yes, they established that a dead acquaintance, whose name they mentioned after many others, was present. Later they talked with others who had died. When they considered a negative answer to be appropriate, they asked the presence to vibrate the needle when the word no was spoken. Questions presented in this manner revealed that the communicant had enjoyed drawing and mathematics while among the living but had not liked mechanics.

A camera was on hand during one experiment, and the communicator indicated that a photograph could be taken of the psychic presence. After the film had been developed and printed, there was no sign that the spirit had been in the room. Another communicator agreed to produce raps for the experimenters. They listened, but no strange sounds, percussive or otherwise, were heard.

Carrington analyzed the detailed report submitted by the two investigators, noting that the method of questioning closely followed Dr. Matla's procedure. He then examined the device his friends had made. It had not been properly insulated. A five-microamperes leakage registered when the switch was thrown. In most cases the needle did not move further until the current from the batteries had heated the various components. Often the force had to be asked many times whether it was prepared to answer questions before an affirmative signal was received. When, by coincidence, the leakage affected the needle, a significant answer was recorded.

Experimenting with several properly insulated systems, Carrington found that the "phenomena" no longer occurred—even when the two spiritualists participated in the tests.

Undaunted by the unsuccessful attempts to duplicate the phenomena described by Dr. Matla, Carrington embarked on another laboratory research venture, patterned after one that had attracted considerable attention in Brussels.

In the summer of 1930 he had been sent a clipping from a London newspaper. It told of a Belgian professor, M. Rutot, who claimed that he had talked with the dead by means of equipment invented by a young man who had died earlier that year. A pair of glass prisms, a dry-cell battery, and a bell were the principal parts of the device.

Professor Rutot, a member of the Royal Academy of Sciences, described his experiments in the July issue of the *Bulletin* of the Conseil des Recherches Métapsychiques de Belgique, but it was not until the next year that a complete description of the apparatus appeared in English in Robert J. Strong's book *Spiritual Engineering.*

Assembled on a flat panel were two glass prisms (one of which had been coated with resin), a triangle made with copper wire, batteries, a bell, and a conductor. Unsheathed copper wire ran from the positive terminal of the batteries to the uncoated prism. Another part of the circuit was a copper wire that extended from the bell close to the base of the triangle.

If the soul or spirit of a dead communicator exerted enough energy toward the prisms, Professor Rutot had written, the force would press the triangle against the unsheathed wire, the circuit would be completed, and the bell would ring. The inventor of the system and the professor contended that energy from a soul generated the electrical charge that closed the gap between the triangle and the wire.

Carrington experimented with wires of various thicknesses. Then he suspended a triangle with a filament taken from a light bulb. For the first series of experiments, which lasted thirty days, the diameter of the wire in the triangle was .25 mm. The tests were not successful. Wire with a .10 mm diameter formed the triangle in another trial. The single door that led to the room had been closed, as well as the window shutters. The sole illumination came from a red bulb. When Carrington asked if a presence that could ring the bell was in the room, there was no response. A repetition of the question caused the bell to sound. Then, on invitation, the presence rang the bell once and three times. Invited to ring the bell only once, the reply was one peal, followed by two more.

When the force was asked to ring if it could answer questions, the bell sounded. When the command was to sound the bell twice, there was no response. Instructions to sound the bell three, five, and four times all produced two peals. The bell rang as erratically during the next experiment as it had previously. Then the apparatus was put in a glass container. Under those conditions the bell did not sound at all.

In his comprehensive report to the members of the American Psychical Institute, Carrington explained how, by induction, wires adjacent to a field of electricity became electrified. Thus an electrostatic area existed between the wire near the triangle and the triangle itself. He quoted from *Spiritual Engineering,* the book that had described Professor Rutot's equipment: "Of course, it (the machine) may not work without a properly instructed spirit operator, any more than a radio station can function without a proper radio engineer." Carrington, however, stated bluntly, "It does not work!" He doubted that any soul or spirit had enough energy to operate the apparatus. No proof had ever been offered "that spirit is in any way directly associated with static electricity, or with a type of electrical charge which is released into the air."

Despite the negative outcome of the experiments that he had made with Dr. Matla's cylinders and the other devices, Carrington had not been dismayed. In his *Laboratory Investigations into Psychic Phenomena* (1939) he stated, "It is my belief that the great discoveries of the present century will be made in the field of psychical research. . . . With adequate support and cooperation such discoveries *can be made!*"

7.

Visitors to
the Afterlife

$\mathbf{D}$r. Raymond A. Moody, Jr.'s *Life After Life* (1975) has universal appeal. Its message is that death should not be dreaded. People who were revived after their hearts had stopped said their pains had ceased and they had found peace. Many claimed to have seen departed loved ones and declared that they had been reluctant to return to their aching bodies.

Dr. Moody wrote that during his ten years of investigation he had often been asked whether he knew of similar cases in the past. He replied that he did not, but that news of them would not surprise him. He may be interested to learn that more than a hundred years before he completed his manuscript several similar instances were cited in Joseph O. Barrett's *Looking Beyond: A Souvenir of Love to the Bereft*. This slender volume, issued in Boston in 1871, was written by a spiritualist.

Like Dr. Moody, Barrett gathered accounts of deathbed visions. For example, E. J. Shelhause described an elder brother's final hours in Colon, Michigan, in June 1848.

The physician, standing by the bedside, carefully examined his patient, and pronounced him 'dead.' At this moment, my oldest brother stepped forward, and placing his arms under the shoulders of the dying brother, raised him to a sitting position and loudly and repeatedly called his name. Calmly he opened his eyes, and for the first time in three weeks, he spoke rational words.

"Why did you call me back," he exclaimed. "I was just going and you called me back. O, what beautiful music I have heard, and such scenes more glorious and beautiful than anything I ever imagined in life. And such throngs of people, with many of whom I was acquainted."

John A. Perry of Elkhorn, Wisconsin, sent Barrett a similar account. Nathanial Bunker, a Quaker, held his mother's hand as she lost consciousness. After her pulse had stopped, she stirred, looked up, and said, "O, Nathanial. Why did you call me back? I have been to heaven."

Another of the author's friends recalled the day his sister died. His distraught mother pleaded for her to return. The child's lips trembled, her eyes opened, and she said in a whisper, "Mother." This happened again. The third and last time, the young girl spoke. She said plaintively, "O, mother, I have been with the angels. I am wanted there. Will you not let me go?"

Barrett described a tragic accident that had taken place in Hingham, Wisconsin, a decade before he wrote his book. Young Kate Marshall had drowned while swimming in the village pond with other girls late one evening. A neighbor, Edward Hobert, hurried to the scene, dived in, and recovered the lifeless body. Pressing on her diaphragm and breathing into her nostrils, he resuscitated her. Kate confessed later that she had not welcomed this reprieve. She had been happy at the bottom of the pond. Her spirit had ascended to join the angels. She had suffered "the most excruciating agonies" as she began to breathe again.

Barrett quotes Samuel Byron Brittan, who in *Man and His Relations* told of an eminent Presbyterian clergyman's encounter with the afterlife. Glowing with light, the minister's spirit rose and hovered over his body. While "thrilled with an inexpressible peace and joy," the minister heard his beloved wife speak his name, and he returned to the still body on the bed.

While the clinically dead patients who recalled their adventures in Moody's more modern book gave few details of the sights they had seen, a forty-one-year-old Rosedale, Kansas, woman provided a comprehensive account of her trip into the unknown more than a century ago. First printed in a Kansas City newspaper, then republished in other American dailies and in spiritualist periodicals, it set a pattern. Alleged spirits, speaking through mediums, were also to describe the heavenly vegetation and houses and the welcome that they had received from loved ones. They too were to speak about how much younger and more vibrant the aged appeared to be and how dead infants had grown to become attractive children.

On August 1, 1876, Mrs. Diana Powellson, a widow whose husband had died several months earlier, leaving her with nine children, cried out that she could not see, as labor pains once more racked her body. The physician in attendance forced her closed lids open and saw that the eyeballs had rolled upward. Beads of perspiration covered her body; eventually she stopped breathing. According to the doctor who was by her side, Mrs. Powellson died at one o'clock the following morning. Attempting to revive her, he sent a current of electricity from the lower part of her brain to the base of her spine. The jolt had no immediate effect. Eventually, however, she recovered. This is the story she told to a reporter.

> On the night I died, I was so happy at going; felt no misery of any kind; pain in the head all gone; it seemed that I lost all consciousness but for a moment; when I came to my senses again I knew I was dead, but everything was very dark to me. I thought I was still blind. I became filled with terror, anticipating the worst. My husband (who died a short time ago), however, took hold of me. Others of my departed family and friends did the same. The darkness suddenly vanished. I saw all my friends and millions of others.
>
> I saw hills and valleys, trees and flowers, rivers, seas, lakes

and birds, and heard such music as I cannot describe. The people were not what I expected to see. They were ordinary men and women. Some were bright and beautiful, and others were lean and miserable looking. I saw their homes. They lived in communities. All were much more beautiful than any we have, but some were not so beautiful as others. I saw many bright spirits, but was very surprised that they had no wings. My friends led me from the dark place into the light. I did not come through this dark place any more, either in coming back or returning at any time. I saw many meetings or congregations, but did not learn what they were doing. I was told that I must return to my body again. My husband told me this. I cried and was very much angered at him and still am for sending me back. I long to be in that beautiful home that they told me was mine.

My husband sent a message to his son and to my children by me. Messages were also sent by many others. I was afraid of some spirits, who looked dark and forbidding, while others were bright, beautiful, and kind. When I was there a large concourse gathered around me. I did not know that I should return to earth till I was told so by my husband. He was sixty-seven when he died, though he now looks in the prime of life. My two children were with their father. I was very much surprised at this; I had known only one; one child was born dead, prematurely. . . . It was quite rejoiced to see me. I cannot compare it with any age, it differs from on earth, but is still a small child. I felt all a mother's love for that child, which I did not think I possessed. My boy, one year old, died fifteen years ago; he is now a young man and knew me.

Spirits do not sing as we do; much nicer. The clothing of all was of the flowing or robe kind. No voice is used by spirits. I understood them more perfectly without words. I read their thoughts; it is more perfect language than ours. They told me to come back to earth for three or four years with my little children who are here. I promised to do so.

I expected to meet Christ, but did not do so. They told me that this was why I was in the dark. I know now that I must depend upon myself. We are over there as we are here. We make our own happiness. I did not find any heaven or hell, only life, more perfect and beautiful than this. This is not life at all. What I now relate is as clear to my memory as anything in life can be. In dying, I did not lose consciousness. I seemed to fade from one life to another. . . .

Spirits told me that they had to repent of their sins over there before they could advance. Till they did this they were unhappy, I was much surprised when I first went there at seeing a spirit which I took to be God, and I afterwards supposed it was Jesus Christ, but who was only a bright spirit teaching the others. I saw many such afterwards; they don't seem to belong to the rest at all. Everybody is engaged in learning and growing brighter, so they told me.

The stories that near-death patients tell of their after-life experiences reflect their interests and backgrounds. Diana Powellson, a Christian, hoped to glimpse God and Christ. Heaven to her was a place where she could live in comfort with her family and friends. The transition was swift and without obstacles.

Contrast this with the account of a physician who obviously had read of a soul-separation process in his studies of occult literature. Dr. A. S. Wiltse, an honorary associate of the American branch of the Society for Psychical Research, believing that he was about to die of typhoid fever, carefully noted how the disease affected his body. His pupils dilated, his vision became hazy, his voice lost its strength, and a heavy feeling depressed him. He tried desperately to extend his legs, brought his arms up to his chest, and interlocked his increasingly stiff fingers.

Soon after he did this, Dr. Wiltse wrote in the November 1889 issue of the *St. Louis Medical and Surgical Journal,* a medical attendant noted that he had stopped breathing. A needle thrust into various parts of his body produced no noticeable reaction. To all appearances, Dr. Wiltse was dead.

The physician, however, wrote that though he lost consciousness for a period, he recovered it in time to be aware of the release of his inner self. There had been a gentle rocking motion, and he heard the snapping of tiny invisible cords inside his feet. His ethereal double moved up and into his head. It skirted the brain and slipped out through the top of the skull. Bobbing up and down like a soap bubble emerging from a pipe, it slipped and fell. Hitting the floor, it expanded and became a duplicate of his physical body. He enjoyed the same elation that others had reported on being released from painful confinements.

Only one thing disturbed him. His second self was as naked as a newborn infant, and there were men and women in the room. His embarrassment was only fleeting, a suit materialized to cover him. He noted with pleasure that he was now taller than he had been in life; he had always regretted being so short. He walked out into the street, but the thin cord extending back to his lifeless body did not break. Apparently it could be stretched to any distance. It was raining, and Wiltse was alone. He had a growing feeling of rejection, for no angel or herald had greeted him.

Then he was raised by invisible hands high above the tree-tops and borne through the air. A massive, menacing dark cloud, bristling with flashes of fire, threatened him. Far below he saw a trio of huge rocks. He knew that beyond the rocks was eternal life—the afterworld.

A voice offered him a choice. If he went to the other side of the three crags, this would indicate that he had completed his mission on earth, and he would never be able to return. Should he have any doubt, he could reenter his physical body. Wiltse went forward, but his decision was not accepted as the right choice. A dark cloud blocked his way, pressing ominously against his face. When he opened his eyes again, he was back in bed.

Those in the room thought that the doctor had expired four hours earlier; Wiltse himself was sure that he had been clinically dead for thirty minutes, perhaps more. As conclusive tests were not made at the time, it is impossible to say just how long the interim period in limbo had lasted.

A more recent visitor to the afterworld told of his impressions in the June 15, 1935, issue of the Detroit *Spiritual Herald*, a monthly. John Puckering, a fifty-eight-year-old patient, had been pronounced clinically dead on a hospital operating table in Birmingham, England.

Puckering said that he had been apprehensive when a gray mist materialized. He floated away behind it. "All at once a bright light shone through the mist and everything became clear to my eyes." He experienced a feeling of peacefulness and happiness. He was aware of "a great array of gleaming pillars, slender and stately and taller than I could see. It was as though I was entering a great hall that had neither walls, ceiling, or floor." The strange gray mist had led him to this place. As he followed it, a brilliant light illuminated the mist, and the gray changed to a rosy hue.

Puckering could make out faces in the haze. "They were rose-cheeked and healthy. They smiled and nodded, as though to make me welcome. I do not recall having seen any bodies beneath the faces, yet I had the impression that the people I saw were dressed very much as people on earth."

He recognized one of the faces smiling through the mist— Walter Whatmore, the postmaster of Puckering's village and five years dead. Seeing the happy postmaster made Puckering realize for the first time that he must himself be dead. Puckering searched for his wife, who had died fifteen years before. He was sure that she was there, but before he could find her, he returned abruptly to the operating table in the Birmingham hospital.

The surgeon, Dr. G. Percival Mills, said later that when Puckering's pulse stopped, every possible means had been used to revive him. The surgeon had inserted his fingers under the diaphragm and was massaging the heart when the patient began to breathe again. Puckering, it was reported, had been clinically dead for five minutes, perhaps longer.

He had not been eager to return to the living. He appreciated the surgeon's skill, but said that all he could look forward to was the prospect of more hard work and the trials of advancing age. "I'm not afraid anymore. I know at least part of what will come after it—and I'll welcome it," he told friends.

Lady Jean Doyle, whose late husband, Sir Arthur Conan Doyle, had gained fame with his Sherlock Holmes stories, shared his belief in the survival of the spirit. "Mr. Puckering's experience," she said, "has been sent to us in order that the people of the world will not fear death, but will realize it is the happiest of birthdays."

In the same issue of the *Spiritual Herald* that carried the Puckering account, Lady Jean expressed her annoyance with mediums who attributed "many useless platitudes" to Sir Arthur in unauthorized messages that they claimed to have received from him. Unless they offered "irrefutable proof that my husband is communicating," she continued, "then we must ask them to refrain from using his name. It is an indefensible thing to use the name of a man, unless by his consent, even in this life, but it is more so when the person is not here to defend himself. Offenses of this nature will be dealt with in a very serious manner." Her efforts, of course, were fruitless. Her husband was to remain a favorite subject for a growing number of mediums, one of the most famous of whom was the Reverend Arthur Ford.

In *Unknown but Known,* published in 1968, three years before his death, Ford recounted an experience he had had while critically ill in a Coral Gables, Florida, hospital. He remembered that a nurse was about to inject a sedative, so that he could sleep without pain. Then he realized that he was floating above the bed, looking down at his body. An interval of unconsciousness followed. He floated to a verdant valley surrounded by mountains. Intense light and brilliant colors awaited him there.

Friends and acquaintances surged toward him. They were not as he remembered them. The aged appeared to be young; children had matured. He was taken on a tour of the area, but did not specify the sights he had seen. When Ford asked about several associates who had died earlier, the bright light dimmed, and the dazzling colors paled. He saw some of these people later in a less developed sphere before he returned to the higher realm to present his admission credentials.

These were not acceptable; he was dispatched back to earth. When he opened his eyes, Ford wrote, a nurse told him that he had been unconscious for two weeks.

Sitting at her typewriter shortly after Ford actually died in 1971, Ruth Montgomery, a former syndicated Washington columnist, who is now a medium, began writing what she called Ford's "eye-witness account of the hereafter." This appeared in her book *A World Beyond* (1971).

According to this source, activities in the afterlife are much the same as those on earth. Ford allegedly told the reporter that he had met Fletcher, who had been his spirit guide, and that he had chatted with two British champions of the psychic cause, Sir Arthur Conan Doyle and Sir Oliver Lodge. Franklin D. Roosevelt and Winston Churchill, Ford observed, were engaged in conversation. Dwight D. Eisenhower had been welcomed by the soldiers who had fought and been killed under his command in World War II. Hitler was there, raving and ranting and being ignored.

Heaven, if we can accept the accounts of those who claim to have been there, is a delightful place, enjoyed by more souls than one would suppose. Reports from hell, which should have a large population, are rare. The communication system there seems not to be working.

8.

Soul Trial in Arizona

A court-approved quest for evidence that a soul leaves the body at death—a search that began after one of the lengthiest legal battles in Arizona history—was instigated and paid for by a missing miner's legacy of more than a quarter of a million dollars.

On the evening of November 8, 1949, James Kidd, a seventy-year-old retired pumpman who had worked in copper-mining camps most of his adult life, borrowed a pick from a friend in Phoenix, saying that he planned to go prospecting in the morning. Where he went or what happened to him is not known. Late in December the prospector's landlord reported to the police that his tenant had disappeared. Kidd's few personal possessions and all of his clothes, except those he had worn, were still in his sparsely furnished, four-dollar-a-week room. His name was not listed on accident or hospital records. He had no known relatives or enemies.

Declared legally dead, he would have been forgotten had not Arizona Estate Tax Commissioner Geraldine C. Swift learned, in investigating his assets, that the recluse who had lived so frugally, patronizing cheap restaurants and smoking five-cent cigars, had by judicious investments accumulated a small fortune. Then, while going through a sheaf of stock-purchase receipts found in an envelope in Kidd's safety-deposit box at the First National Bank in Phoenix, she discovered a handwritten document.

Scrawled on a torn blue-ruled ledger page, dated Phoenix, Arizona, January 2, 1946, were the words "This is my first and only will." The message was short and explicit.

> I have no heirs and have not been married in my life and after all my funeral expenses have been paid and . . . one hundred dollars to some preacher of the gospitel [sic] to say fare well at my grave sell all my property which in cash and stocks with E. F. Hutton Co. Phoenix some in safety deposit box, and have this balance money to go in a research [f]or some scientific proof of a soul of the human body which leaves at death. I think in time there can be a photograph of soul leaving the human at death. James Kidd

Apparently as an afterthought, he had added "some cash in Valley bank some in Bank America LA Cal." Despite the erratic punctuation, misspellings, and awkward constructions, the meaning was clear.

Judge Robert L. Meyers presided over the Superior Court of Maricopa County in Phoenix on March 11, 1964, the day that Estate Tax Commissioner Swift and Assistant Attorney General Robert Murlless offered opposing views on the will. She contended that it was a valid legal document. He disagreed, arguing that the money should be assigned to the state treasury as unclaimed property. Even before the court announced that it had accepted the will for probate, a rumor spread that almost two hundred thousand dollars would be awarded to the person or organization best qualified to conduct the required research.

The first of the more than 130 claimants for the missing miner's bonanza was a Phoenix group headed by the Reverend Richard T. Ireland. The University of Life Church, Inc., so the petition read, had been formed to investigate "the Phenomena of Spirit Return," to conduct "discussions, classes, séances, spirit communications," and to proclaim "the truths of conscious immortality of the soul." Ireland, while blindfolded and holding questions written by members of the congregation, gave answers allegedly transmitted to him by the dead. Later he was to present this routine in nightclubs and cabarets.

Though the lost prospector had said he had no heirs, Herman Silas Kidd and John Herbert Kidd, two Canadians in their eighties, claimed him as their long-lost brother; a New York woman said she had been married to the miner; and two Wisconsin sisters professed to be his daughters. The most interesting of the hundreds of letters addressed to the superior-court judge did not come from a claimant. One paragraph explained why the words were typed: The writer's hand had been injured in an accident. Another paragraph said that the writer had always wondered what someone would do to get "a large amount of money." He hoped that it would be given to a "worthy person." He himself was now using an assumed name. The last four typed words were "Quite alive, James Kidd."

The only contender for the Kidd estate to state that the miner was present during the hearings was Nora Higgins. She had traveled to Phoenix from Branscomb, California, to stake her claim in person. She had not met Kidd until he died. He materialized in her bedroom in 1964. She said his spirit double was pacing back and forth in the courtroom, making comments on the case.

The Right Reverend Robert Raleigh, bishop of the Thousand Oaks, California, Antioch Church, did not comment on the prospector's presence, but said a visitor from outer space, who traveled in a spacecraft to Malabra, California, in 1949, had informed him that earlier explorers had flown to earth two million years previously.

Dr. Gardner Murphy, president of the American Society for Psychical Research, took the witness stand on June 6, 1967. Asked about the society's investigations of soul survival, the distinguished psychologist mentioned studies of crisis apparitions—descriptions, by people not on the scene, of the deaths of loved ones; deathbed accounts of the afterlife reported by nurses and doctors; and physical phenomena linked with the time of death—such as the sudden stopping of a clock.

Questioned as to how a link between these manifestations and a departing soul might be established, Dr. Murphy replied that an algometer could indicate whether pressure had been applied to a surface. Sound equipment and cameras might record other "registerable effects." He thought "it might be very interesting to show what happens at the moment of death involving some spatial separation of psychic events from the physical body which can make a physical mark somewhere."

Another area that should be thoroughly investigated concerned out-of-the-body experiences. Many people claimed that they had left their bodies, traveled to distant places, and then returned. There was no scientific proof that these astral journeys had been made. Instruments at a target point could register if something there had been seen, heard, or touched.

Asked whether, if the society received two hundred thousand dollars for the purpose specified in Kidd's will, proof would be produced that a soul survives death, Dr. Murphy answered, "No, proof is much too strong a word."

Jean Bright, a widow from Encino, California, who claimed that a dead dentist caused the muscles of her head and legs to twitch, questioned Dr. Murphy about his personal beliefs. "Do you think that it is possible that someone in the court may have proof which is not known to the sensitives and is not known to you personally, and there could be a breakthrough?" He replied, "The word 'possible' I would certainly admit." Neither she nor anyone else asked him about a statement he had made in his *Challenge of Psychical Research* (1961). "Trained as a psychologist, and now in my sixties, I do not actually anticipate finding myself in existence after physical death."

Others were more positive about the soul and its function. William A. Dennis, a Balboa, California, geophysicist, held that cosmic vibrations were centered in the soul. These unseen influences enabled a human to think. After the body died, the vibrations did not cease. Lieutenant Colonel Virsat W. Ambudha, an officer in the Thai army, flew from Bangkok to explain that the soul and the mind are synonymous. If he won the award, he would publish his theories in a text, which he would distribute throughout the world.

Richard Carl Spurney, philosophy teacher at Mount San Antonio Junior College, came from Walnut, California, to give the court an illustrated lecture on the difference between the mind and the brain, displaying fruit and a television set as he talked about the former and a can of spaghetti to represent the latter. When an intellect charged through the spaghetti of the brain it became a mind or a soul!

Lyle Hartford Van Dyke, Jr., of Portland, Oregon, stated that as a result of his twelve-year study of gravitation and theoretical physics he was qualified to undertake the research that the lost miner had envisioned.

More qualified, at least as a research center, in the opinion of many observers, was the Barrow Neurological Institute at St. Joseph's Hospital in Phoenix. Grants from the National Science Foundation, the United States Department of Health, the United States Navy and other donors had financed scientific and medical studies of the nervous system in the institute's laboratories. Electro-recording devices with microelectrodes, an electronic microscope with an amplification capacity of some sixty-thousand times, and an isolation chamber where light, sound, vibrations, and odors from the outside could be blocked were among its many facilities.

Representatives of the institute (and the Neurological Sciences Foundation, which raised funds for it) told about their many achievements in a highly specialized field, but did not consider soul to be a scientifically acceptable term. They had never studied the possible survival of human personality and did not offer an outline of experiments in this area that could be conducted in the future.

The Arizona Board of Regents, applying for the legacy to endow a Northern Arizona University chair of philosophy, also made it clear that they had no intention of sponsoring soul-separation tests. They were willing to endorse a discus-

sion program covering various concepts of what a soul might
be.

From the start there had been a clash between those who
willingly gave their own definitions of a soul and those who
avoided this issue. The Barrow Neurological Institute had
been established so that more could be learned about life
processes. By contrast, the Psychical Research Foundation
in Durham, North Carolina, had been formed to study the
possibility that the human personality somehow survives after
death.

Founded in 1960 by Charles E. Ozanne, a teacher who
earlier had contributed to similar groups, the Psychical Research Foundation did not probe the entire psychic spectrum.
Project director William G. Roll limited investigations to phenomena that seemed to have some relation to survival—poltergeist disturbances, for example. He thought that the dis-
ruptive forces that sometimes wreak havoc in houses might
be disembodied personalities, not rebellious youngsters, dis-
gruntled employees, or malicious troublemakers, as skeptics
have suggested.

Dr. Joseph Gaither Pratt, president of the board of direc-
tors of the Psychical Research Foundation, had worked at
J. B. Rhine's Duke University Parapsychology Laboratory.
Now a staff researcher with the parapsychology unit at the
University of Virginia School of Medicine, he testified that
the Psychical Research Foundation, because of its specialized
interests, could carry out the intent of the Kidd will effectively.

Dr. Ian Stevenson, another member of the Psychical Research Foundation board, also journeyed to Phoenix to endorse its eligibility. A year earlier Chester F. Carlson, inventor
of Xerography and head of the Xerox Corporation, had endowed a research professorship in psychiatry at the University
of Virginia. Dr. Stevenson, chairman of the Department of
Neuropsychiatry at the School of Medicine, had been chosen
by Carlson for this post. Dr. Stevenson assured the court
that most of his future investigations would be in the field

of parapsychology and that he would continue to be a board member of the Durham organization.

Fifteen years earlier, Dr. Stevenson testified, he had started gathering stories of people who claimed to have lived before. Since then he had traveled to Alaska, Europe, Turkey, Thailand, Ceylon, and India to interview and assess those who professed to have memories of previous existences. Most were children. He had written a book on the subject, *Twenty Cases Suggestive of Reincarnation* (1966).

When Dr. Gardner Murphy had been asked about reincarnation and resurrection, he had replied that the latter, in the sense of "actual returns to the physical body," was to the best of his knowledge not an area explored by psychical research. There was evidence for reincarnation; he cited Dr. Stevenson's book. Then he stressed that this was "evidence, not proof."

Only one attempt was made to convince the court that reincarnation proved that the soul survived. A Congregational clergyman from Princeton, New Jersey, the Reverend Franklin Loehr, chief research investigation officer of the Religious Research Foundation of America, believed that General Charles de Gaulle was a reincarnation of Napoleon Bonaparte. DeGaulle's reluctance to invite Great Britain into the European Common Market, Loehr explained, stemmed from Napoleon's resentment of his defeat at the Battle of Waterloo by the Duke of Wellington.

Though Emma Georgia Clausser, a Riverside, California, petitioner, claimed that she had seen her soul detached from her body and had observed "its form, shape, color, and structure," she did not offer to show the soul-separation process to the court. Another Californian, Dr. Joseph W. Still, like many other contenders, seemed more interested in presenting a theory than in justifying a claim to the legacy. The Los Angeles physician stated that there were three types of death: organic, psychic, and vegetable. The soul departed after psychic death. Once it was gone, the body became a vegetable. Though the heart beat, and respiration occurred, without the soul, the body was not really alive.

The Reverend Russell Dilts presented photographic evidence that the missing miner had appeared in the spirit. The photograph showed a picture allegedly materialized during a séance at Camp Chesterfield, an Indiana spiritist center. In the picture were ten images—one resembling James Kidd.

The June-to-September hearings ended with no hint as to the outcome of the soul case. Those who claimed to be heirs had been disqualified. Judge Myers had also ruled out petitions that were theological rather than, in at least some sense, scientific. He had listened to philosophical discussions and had heard of feats that seemed to be beyond comprehension. He delivered his verdict on October 20, 1967.

James Kidd, he wrote, had intended that "his estate be used for the purpose of research which may lead to some scientific proof of a soul of the individual human which leaves the body at death. . . . Such research can best be done in the combined fields of medical science, psychiatry and psychology, and can best be performed and carried on by the Barrow Neurological Institute, Phoenix, Arizona."

John G. Fuller, the author of *Incident at Exeter* and other books dealing with the fantastic, flew to Phoenix four months after Judge Myers had delivered his decision. In *The Great Soul Trial* (1969) Fuller noted that "several of the parapsychology groups" were planning to contest the verdict. Then in an article, "$233,000 . . . for a Soul Search," which appeared in the April 1968 issue of *Fate* magazine, editor Mary Margaret Fuller quoted one of the disappointed claimants, Fred B. Nordstrom, who had been considering joining with other petitioners in an appeal to a higher court: "It is regrettable," the Chicago engineer lamented, "that the winner of an amount approximately four times as large as the Nobel Prize should be chosen from a group some of whose answers to questions asked in court were ambiguous and whose proposed methods of research were also ambiguous."

Nordstrom eventually decided not to pursue the matter. Two men and two organizations appealed Judge Myers's decision. The men—Dr. Joseph W. Still, who had studied the dying process, and the Reverend Russell Dilts, who had displayed the Camp Chesterfield spirit likeness of Kidd—and the organizations—the American Society for Psychical Research and the Psychical Research Foundation—contended that the Barrow Neurological Institute had no intention of using the miner's money for a soul search, the purpose specified in the will. Fred Stuckmeyer, chief justice of the Arizona Supreme Court, reversed the finding of the lower court in February 1971 and directed that the legacy be awarded by the Superior Court of Maricopa County to one or more of the claimants contesting the decision.

The two parapsychology groups joined forces. The American Society for Psychical Research outlined how the money would be spent in scientific soul investigations if the court found in its favor. Two-thirds of the sum would be allotted to the older society, the remaining third to the Psychical Research Foundation.

This proved to be a sound strategy. On December 29, 1972—more than eight years after Judge Myers had first seen the will and more than five years after his initial verdict—the Kidd estate, by then amounting to $270,000, was awarded to the American Society for Psychical Research and the probe for that intangible something that James Kidd referred to as a soul began.

9.

Out-of-the-Body
on West 73rd Street

Not one of the 270,000 dollars of the James Kidd estate awarded to the American Society for Psychical Research by the Superior Court of Maricopa County, Arizona, was to be spent for the purpose specified by the missing miner's will. Kidd had written that he wanted "a research [f]or some scientific proof of a soul of the human body which leaves at death." He had also hoped that a photograph could be taken of the soul as it ascended.

The research schedule, published in the Spring 1973 *ASPR Newsletter* listed three areas of investigation: "1. Research on Ecsomatic [out-of-the-body] Experiences of Living Persons, 2. Transcultural Study of Deathbed Experiences, 3. Studies on Bio-electric Phenomena."

Even if it could be shown that the consciousness of a *living* subject had been projected out of a body, this would not prove that a soul leaves the body at death. Nor could an analysis of deathbed testimonies scientifically establish it; at best this would be a census of mental images described by the dying and reported by doctors and nurses—hearsay evidence that no court of law would accept.

The only proposed test that approached the Kidd mandate was one "to measure changes in the bio-electrical field surrounding living organisms, including changes associated with the process of dying." The schedule did not say that this experiment would be carried out, but that "an exploration will be made of the feasibility of utilizing certain new techniques."

Had an alert attorney for one of the other 133 claimants to the Kidd legacy noted that only one scientific experiment involving "the process of dying" had been planned, and only tentatively at that, a petition to the probate court might have stopped this expenditure of the lost prospector's money.

The soul had not been mentioned in the brief reference to the possible bio-electrical probe. Soul was a term to be avoided at the American Society for Psychical Research, as it had been at the Barrow Neurological Institute in Phoenix. Consider these words preceding the research plan in the *ASPR Newsletter:*

> James Kidd's will indicates that his main concern was research on the "soul" which is capable of leaving the body at the moment of death. However, the dominant viewpoint of contemporary scientific thought considers human personality to be a psychophysiological whole; the body, especially the brain, being inseparable from human personality and its mental and spiritual activities. If this is true, then there is nothing in the human organism capable of leaving the body at death for continued existence.

Having sidestepped the soul issue, the society decided to test the hypothesis that personality could function when projected from a living body in an upstairs room at their headquarters on West 73rd Street in Manhattan. Though the Kidd money was not received until late December 1972, it had been awarded in July 1971, and exploratory out-of-the-body experience (OOBE) experiments were soon designed.

Ingo Swann, identified as "our major subject" in the Summer 1972 *ASPR Newsletter* and as "our star OOBE experient" in the Autumn issue, frequently amazed the research staff with his strange demonstrations. Swann, a tall, hefty Coloradan in his late thirties, had progressed from mysticism to

Scientology in the early 1960s, while working in the communications center at the United Nations in New York City. Born in Telluride, a small town in the Rocky Mountains, he said that he had had his first out-of-the-body experience several months before his third birthday, while anesthetized by ether previous to having his tonsils removed. His consciousness hovered above the operating table as the surgeon's scalpel accidently nicked his physical tongue. He heard the doctor swear and saw where the tonsils were put after being removed.

Swann had majored in art and biology at Westminster College in Salt Lake City, Utah, before serving three years with the Army in eastern Asia. Finding it impossible to earn enough to live as an artist in Manhattan after his return to the United States, Swann found a job at the United Nations. While there, he joined L. Ron Hubbard's Church of Scientology, paid several thousand dollars to clear his mind of emotional blocks, and later reached the highest possible point of development, by Hubbard standards—Operational Thetan-VII. One of the many powers said to be possessed by Thetans in this category is the ability to project their consciousness to distant places.

Swann's consciousness did not have to travel far during the out-of-the-body experiments in the American Society for Psychical Research's brownstone on West 73rd Street. Dr. Karlis Osis, the director of research, wrote in the Summer 1972 *ASPR Newsletter* that Swann, "attached to a polygraph (in another room) which records data concerning his physiological state, i.e. brain waves (EEG), heart rate, respiration, etc.," sat in a "semi-dark" test chamber. Out of view on a shelf suspended two feet below the ceiling were several objects. Swann's task was to describe and illustrate these targets as his detached consciousness perceived them.

In *To Kiss Earth Good-bye* (1975) Swann tells in detail about an experiment made three years earlier on the afternoon of January 12. The room was not, as Dr. Osis had reported, "semi-dark." It was illuminated by "two kitchen-style fixtures overhead." As Swann sat in a chair with the wires from electrodes fastened to his head running through the wall behind him, he stared at the far wall. Hanging on it was a large painting of a sea scene. To one side was a smaller painting of flowers and to the other was a reproduction of Vincent Van Gogh's *Sowers,* the only thing in the room that did not offend Swann's artistic sensibilities.

Dr. Osis had written that the shelf was two feet below the ceiling; Swann added that it was "several feet" above his head. He smoked a cigar as he waited for the signal to— as he preferred to call it—exteriorize. When the signal came, almost effortlessly he viewed the target. His psychic vision, he admitted, was not as keen as his normal sight. Yet he perceived something black and long resting on a red, round-ish form on one section of the shelf and what seemed to be a sharpshooter's target on the other. Picking up a clip-board, he quickly sketched these objects. The test was completed in precisely one minute.

When the objects were removed from the shelf, he saw how accurate his psychic peek had been. Resting on a large red heart was a black letter opener and scissors case, and what had seemed to be a target was—a target!

Commenting on eight Swann sessions, Dr. Osis wrote that a psychologist had been given the objects viewed and Swann's responses. She had matched all correctly. The odds on scoring so high, Dr. Osis stressed, were about forty thousand to one. The physiological data had not as yet been thoroughly evaluated. "The autonomic nervous system responses seem quite within normal range." Brain-wave readings had not been analyzed, "but the voltage changes do appear to be important," Dr. Osis wrote.

Swann's out-of-the-body travels became more extensive. He projected his consciousness into outer space and painted what he saw on his astral journeys. Seven of these canvases were on display at the reception that the American Society for Psychical Research held for their outstanding exteriorizer on April 26, 1972. "As I have developed my own ability to 'exteriorize,'" he commented, "the experience has begun to reveal itself cogently as one of the most astonishing potentialities of mankind. . . . Becoming aware of greater and greater magnitudes of complexity, I have felt the need to set up for myself metaphysical and ethical standards to govern the use and development of this ability.''

The society's receipt of the Kidd legacy in 1971 had produced more publicity than it had received in years. A hundred new members signed up in a single month. Now that an expert in out-of-the-body travel had been found, interest in the oldest organization of its kind in the United States continued to mount. Yet there were members, the present writer for one, who were disappointed that so little information had been printed in the society's publications about the out-of-the-body sessions. What precautions had been taken against possible fraud?

Some possibilities for deception had been listed by Dr. Charles T. Tart, a psychologist at the University of California at Davis, in "A Psychophysiological Study of Out-of-the-Body Experiences in a Selected Subject," which appeared in the January 1968 issue of the *Journal of the American Society for Psychical Research.* His experiment seems to have been the inspiration for the tests in New York.

Tart's subject was a former college student who said that she often awoke at night with her consciousness high above her sleeping physical self. Dr. Tart advised her to mix paper slips numbered from one to ten in a box, then to put one of them, without glancing at the number, on a bedside table. The slip was to be in a position where the number could not be sighted from the bed, but could be read from above. When the subject left her body, she was to read and remember the number; in the morning she was to see whether that number tallied with the one on the paper.

She reported that she had succeeded seven times. Dr. Tart invited her to spend four nights in his sleep laboratory. There were two rooms with a door and a large observation window in the dividing wall. A partially closed venetian blind at the window permitted some light to enter the sleep chamber.

The young woman rested on a bed beneath the window.

The wires from electrodes attached to her head extended to terminals that permitted her to turn, but if she raised her head "more than two feet," the electrode leads would be pulled from their sockets. Five feet and six inches over her head was a shelf. Above this was a large wall clock.

After the subject seemed to be asleep, Dr. Tart wrote a randomly selected five-digit number on a sheet of paper with a black marking pen, each digit about two inches tall. He placed the paper, writing side up, on the shelf in the sleep chamber and returned to the adjacent room.

There he monitored the polygraph and, listening through an intercom, jotted down the words spoken by the subject. He noted that near the end of the session the subject woke up, saying that she had floated up to the shelf to see the target number. She called out a five-digit number. It was the one Dr. Tart had written. This, he said, "was the first strong evidence that her OOB experiences contained a parapsychological element."

Was there any way in which the woman could have seen what was on the shelf? Dr. Tart reported that the shelf was about five feet, six inches above the reclining subject's head and that the slack in the electrode wires would permit her to raise her head two feet. This leaves a gap of three and a half feet to be spanned. If the woman had brought her knees under her body, turned and raised her right shoulder above her head, bracing herself with her left hand on the bed, her right shoulder would have been some six inches closer to the shelf. If she had then extended her right arm upwards to its full length, her fingers could have been less than ten inches from the shelf. If she had held a mirror with a handle in her right hand, by tilting the mirror and looking up she could have seen a reflection of the paper on the shelf.

Dr. Tart himself noted in his article, which was revised for Edgar D. Mitchell's *Psychic Exploration* (1974): that the woman "might have concealed a mirror and telescoping rod in her pajamas" and peeked at the shelf "when she thought I might not be looking through the observation window."

The woman had not been searched prior to the experiment,

nor had an observer been in the sleep chamber with her—precautions that should have been taken. Dr. Tart admitted in his article, but not in the book, that "occasionally *I dozed* during the night beside the equipment." (Italics added) Could the subject have known when the parapsychologist was napping? Yes—the room in which he sat was lit, and she could see, as he himself did, through the partially open slats of the venetian blind on the window between the two rooms.

It should be noted that Dr. Tart wrote the target digits about two inches high "with a black marking pen." The large size would make it easier for the subject to see them—if trickery was used.

Another possibility for cheating—mentioned in Dr. Tart's article but excluded from the book—was that the number might have been reflected by the glass face of the wall clock above the shelf. The day after the experiment, Dr. Tart and a colleague attempted to make out a reflected number from the subject's bed. Neither could see a reflection without additional light on the paper. Nonetheless, when preparing for a second test with the same woman, Dr. Tart extended the shelf to make such a glimpse impossible. However, she left the city before a follow-up experiment could be made.

In the tests with Swann in New York, the subject also was alone in the chamber with the target. Although his outstretched arm might not have extended far enough to reach the suspended shelf the clipboard that he used for sketching could have been employed as an extension if a mirror had been held up by the clip and the lower end of the clipboard grasped by the fingers of the extended hand.

In his book Swann wrote that while he was aware of most of the objects on the shelf above his head, he did not know that it also held four numbers. A photograph, reproduced in his book, of the target objects on the shelf indicates that the numbers were all at one side, a side that would not, it seems, have been readily visible if a reflecting surface had been angled near that end.

Why, one wonders, were the targets for an out-of-the-body

test in the same room with the subject? Why were they so close to the subject? Why was an observer not in the room with the subject when the experiment was made?

Dr. Osis reported on a new series of out-of-the-body tests, termed "fly-ins," in the Summer 1974 *ASPR Newsletter.* A well-publicized appeal for volunteers who believed that they could leave their bodies whenever they chose to and travel to specific locations at specified times, produced far more applicants than had been expected.

More than a hundred volunteers had been tested. Before a scheduled "fly-in," target objects, randomly selected, were arranged on a table in Dr. Osis's office. Participants had been told to view the objects, when their separated personalities entered the room, from a position in front of the fireplace.

From questionnaires filled in by the invisible visitors after they had returned to their bodies, Dr. Osis gathered some fascinating data. Take-offs made while sitting were as effective as those made while reclining. The exteriorizers who blanked out suddenly and then regained consciousness on arrival in the office scored higher than those who remained fully aware of the separation process, or those who made detours en route and did not land directly in the place previously designated.

Subjects who had to wrench their personalities from their bodies and those who experienced difficulties in getting back into them were handicapped by these problems. Few fliers who said that they were constantly aware of both their mental and physical selves were able to sight the targets clearly. Just how successful each "fly-in" had been was not reported. "The over-all results," Dr. Osis stated, "were not significant."

Though the director of research had not been fortunate enough to see either the out-of-the-body visitors to his office or any manifestations that indicated an invisible presence, an aide, Bonnie Perskari, had observed "a ball of light and a blue mist." A medium there at the time also attested to these phenomena.

While preparations were being made to photograph and

videotape another "fly-in," Bonnie Perskari picked up a camera and snapped several pictures. Minutes later, the woman whose psychic arrival had been scheduled telephoned to complain that a flashbulb had been fired under her astral nose. Did an image appear on the film? Dr. Osis doesn't know. The camera, he said, was stolen before the film could be removed and processed.

Two impressive testing machines were installed for new out-of-the-body vision experiments. One, an "Optical Image Device," was housed in a two- by two- by three-foot structure. When a researcher switched on a mechanism, a disk, divided into four equal sections like a pie, revolved. Each quarter bore a different color.

One of five symbols, randomly selected by the machine, appeared on a colored quadrant, also chosen by chance when the wheel stopped turning. The operator of the machine did not learn until later which symbols, colors, or quadrants were involved in an experiment. This data could be decoded from an automatic recording machine. Unless someone—or a disembodied personality—looked through a small window at the front of the structure, the target image could not be seen.

The second new device featured a "Color Wheel" similar to those at roulette tables. When this fourteen-inch spinning circle was stopped mechanically by chance, a target symbol in color stood out against a black surface. Only by peeking down through an opening at the top of the box could the complete image be perceived.

This machine, like the first, had been designed to preclude the leakage of telepathic clues from an experimenter to a subject. According to Dr. Osis, one subject, Alex Tanous, had learned, after many failures, how to evaluate his out-of-the-body vision scores before they were announced. Tanous, Dr. Osis said, visualized his consciousness as a hazy luminous cloud. When the light focused on a dime-sized area, Tanous was sure he would be successful.

An experiment of a different sort centered on a weight suspended by a string in "an enclosed, electrically isolated space." Dr. Osis called this a "Diving Pool." Volunteers, forty feet away in a soundproof chamber, attempted to move the pendulum by projecting their personalities into the enclosure. Jim Merewether, a physicist who monitored these sessions, reported minimal action on the polygraph chart recording the pendulum's movements during exploratory tests. Pat Price, a retired California police official, caused the electronic instrument to fluctuate wildly during his first visit. In later trials only an eighth of the initial variance was noted. Nonetheless Dr. Osis stated that "a real breakthrough" might be made.

None of these out-of-the-body experiments can be properly evaluated; complete data about them have never been published. Nor has the vital information about all of the earlier Ingo Swann sessions appeared in print.

It is regrettable that the society which was awarded $270,000 to probe for scientific proof "of a soul of the human body which leaves at death" has not issued a full account of its out-of-the-body investigations. Even so, it is hard to understand just what the ASPR thought it was proving, since tests of personality projections by living subjects appear to have little bearing on the question of whether a soul leaves a *dying* body.

10.

Consciousness
Projection in Durham

In January 1973 the Psychical Research Foundation
in Durham, North Carolina, received a grant from the American Society for Psychical Research, amounting to approximately a third of the $270,000 legacy of James Kidd, whose
will had specified that his estate be used in a search for scientific evidence of a soul. Dr. Robert L. Morris, research coordi-
nator for the foundation, outlined its approach to the problem. If the Theta Aspect (the foundation's term for soul)
of a human survived death, it was likely a part of the body
before death and probably responsible for the paranormal
experiences of the living.

Probes would be made in two categories, Dr. Morris announced in the Summer 1973 issue of the *ASPR Newsletter:*
out-of-the-body projections and hauntings. Reports of haunt-
ing incidents, "especially those which suggest spatially and
temporally discrete phenomena," were being gathered and
would be compared with data recorded during out-of-the-
body experiments.

Measurements of brain-wave fluctuations, respiration rates,
and other psychophysiological variations might reveal that
the condition of the body during consciousness projection
was the same as, or similar to, its state while dreaming. An

effort would be made to verify the presence of a projected consciousness at target areas with animal, human, and instrumental detectors.

No one read Dr. Morris's plan of action with greater interest than Blue Harary, the Psychical Research Foundation's resident out-of-the-body traveler. The bearded, bushy-haired, Brooklyn-born Duke University undergraduate had allegedly been slipping out of his body periodically for eight years. Shy as a youngster, he had been most at ease with invisible friends. He talked with them, told them his problems, and heeded their advice.

When he was twelve, Blue claimed later, he had learned how to become invisible himself. He said that one night he had drifted away from his body accidentally. Enjoying the feeling of weightlessness and freedom, he had mastered the launching and reentry techniques.

Harary's parents had called him Stuart, but his unseen friends told him that his real name was Blue. Thereafter, that was the name he preferred. While a student at Nebraskan Wesleyan University, he returned to New York for a holiday in the winter of 1971. There he visited the headquarters of the American Society for Psychical Research and told Janet Mitchell, a staff member, about his psychic adventures. She invited him to participate in the out-of-the-body tests made possible by the Kidd legacy. Unlike Ingo Swann, the confident star of the early bilocation experiments, Blue was hesitant. However, he later returned to the building on West 73rd Street and reluctantly submitted to what he thought would be an ordeal. He recalled this venture for David Black, whose fascinating book *Ekstasy: Out-of-the-Body Experiences* was published in 1975.

Asked to project himself to an upstairs room in the brownstone, Blue said he saw there "a rectangular box with wires, and on front of that a circle with an X in it. A statuette. And antlers." Even Dr. Karlis Osis, the director of research, showed a trace of excitement at this. A statue of an antlered deer was in the target room. The "rectangular box with wires" was identified as a tape machine. The "circle with an X in it" turned out to be a plastic reel on the recorder. In this, as in most reels, were four triangular openings at the top and bottom, so that the user could see how much tape was on the spool. The remaining plastic formed "a circle with an X in it."

The following summer Blue projected his consciousness to a shelf over his head in a laboratory room and attempted to peer with the eyes of his detached self into openings of boxes in other rooms some distance away. How well he scored is a matter of conjecture, since a report on his efforts has yet to be published.

In the fall Blue entered Duke University as a psychology major. He explained why in a letter to Marian Nester, editor of the *ASPR Newsletter*, published in the Autumn 1973 issue. Students who planned to work in the field of parapsychology should "attend colleges or universities that were close to research centers." Dr. J. B. Rhine's Foundation for Research on the Nature of Man and the Psychical Research Foundation were only a few minutes from the Duke campus.

By the time this letter appeared in print Blue had achieved one of his aims; he was a research assistant at the Psychical Research Foundation.

The advent of Blue Harary solved a dilemma that had plagued the foundation. Many people had claimed to have had one or more out-of-the-body experiences, but they could not trigger them at will. Some of those who volunteered for preliminary procedures were so disturbed by the electrodes pasted to their skin that they could not calm down and project; others admitted that their previous flights had been induced by narcotics. Blue, however, seemingly could release his consciousness from restraining physical bonds as readily as Houdini had escaped from standard handcuffs.

Blue lived in one of the three buildings on the foundation's property. Sometimes an experiment called for him to project himself from a laboratory at Duke, a quarter of a mile away, to the foundation target area; sometimes he relaxed in a room at the foundation fifty feet distant from the site he was to visit invisibly. He had to avoid mental tensions and could unwind by taking a brisk walk and a bath. Sometimes he meditated before the electrodes attached to a multitape polygraph were applied. If an unexpected delay arose, he occasionally visualized himself in the target room. These mental pictures could be so realistic that only with great difficulty could he restrain his consciousness from departing immediately.

William G. Roll, project director of the Psychical Research Foundation, tells about Harary's attempts to identify large letters of the alphabet of various colors displayed in the target room in the paper he contributed to Edgar D. Mitchell's *Psychic Exploration.* According to Roll, Blue's descriptions of colors were "close to the actual one" in "five of nine calls"; in three instances he gave the shape of a letter, but not the letter itself.

In one test Blue, after mentioning several shapes, spoke about an *s,* similar to "an *n* on its side." The letter in this case was a *z.* He described an oval when the target was a *q,* and a *v,* "or something with a long diagonal," when a *w* had been hanging on the wall. Even so, Harary's responses were not above the level of chance.

On the possibility that Blue might be more accurate if the targets were human, another series of tests began, involving three people and three positions in the target room. Blue was told that as many as three persons or as few as one would be at a location. He zeroed in accurately with his first two tries, but his score declined during the six that followed.

An object observation test not included in the formal experiments was staged by D. Scott Rogo, a visiting parapsychologist from California, one summer night in 1973. Rogo, a foundation consultant, had had out-of-the-body experiences himself. He arranged for Harary and Dr. Morris to go to a lab at Duke Hospital; then he placed several objects in or near a circular cage in a target area in a foundation building.

Blue telephoned to report what he had seen: "Round flat object like plate . . . maybe glass . . . something black and square diagonally . . . two things both might have been the same thing . . . something tall standing middle. Might have created a kitten. Long pencil on top. Something round. Not the piece of wood, maybe a Frisbee on top. Maybe saw bottle. Shoe on top." Dr. Morris wrote the words as Blue spoke them.

Rogo tells what the targets were in *In Search of the Unknown* (1976). He had taken his oboe to Durham. He put the open black instrument case with the oboe resting on it inside the circular cage. Behind the cage he had constructed a bottle sandwich—a large bottle between two plastic Frisbees. Though neither a kitten nor a shoe had been targets, Blue's rambling descriptive phrases could be tied to the targets used. And he had specifically said "Frisbee."

Eager to experiment further, Rogo assembled a new group of targets. A summer electrical storm threatened to disrupt the proceedings, as Blue did not like to project his personality through bolts of lightning. Yet he braved the elements and again reported that he had visited the target site. He made a successful prediction: He said that, as he had not been able to see the objects clearly, this test would be a fiasco. It was.

Rogo believes that Blue's consciousness possibly paid him a surprise visit early in the morning of the parapsychologist's next-to-last day in Durham. Rogo had been restless the night before. At 3:22 A.M. the "half-awake" investigator saw a luminous red ball streak from one side of his bedroom to the other.

If the red ball was a manifestation of Harary's soul, Rogo was a far better detector than most of the animals used for this purpose in a Psychical Research Foundation target area. A hamster and some gerbils gave no observable or measureable indications that Blue's detached personality interested or disturbed them. A snake became active during one test period, remaining almost motionless during others.

Someone suggested that a dog would be more alert and responsive. The dog brought in for a preliminary experiment fell asleep. Two kittens purchased from the same litter and cared for by Harary showed more promise. Blue named them

Spirit and Soul. Though less than three months old, they exhibited no tendency to nap while a test was in progress.

Reporting on the animal detector activities in the Summer 1974 issue of *Theta,* the foundation's periodical, Dr. Morris wrote that the kittens had been put in a topless box, thirty-six inches high, eighty inches long, and thirty inches wide. The floor of the box had been marked with two dozen ten-inch squares. As the squares were numbered, the movements of the animals could be graphed.

Spirit and Soul explored the box during the first preliminary observation period. During the second, Spirit stopped prowling. This was significant, as the kitten became calm and ceased meowing at the very time that Blue was projecting himself to the area. Thereafter Spirit was placed in the box alone. Harary had been told to project himself twice in each test for a two-minute stay. During two control segments, also two minutes long, he was to divert his attention elsewhere. The times for these hot and cold activities were randomly selected.

The results, to use a phrase employed by enthusiastic but cautious parapsychologists, warranted further investigation. In the course of eight tests Spirit moved restlessly from one square to another, except when Blue's personality was scheduled to be in the area. More intriguing was the meow factor. Spirit had meowed thirty-seven times in all, but not once when Harary had been projecting.

This consistent behavior of the kitten detector encouraged the researchers to plan an orientation experiment in which Spirit was to have the star role. A round cage, two feet tall and thirty-four inches in diameter, which had been designed for another, unrelated experiment, was placed in a central location in a foundation building. The floor of this cage was composed of eight wedge-shaped portions. The movement of the animal from one wedge to another would stop and start two of the eight timing mechanisms in another room.

Four places north, east, south, and west of the container were to be target locations. Blue, wired to a polygraph in a distant laboratory, was to project his consciousness to one of those locations. In theory, the kitten, sensing Harary's arrival, would go in that direction.

Before each test Blue signaled that he was ready to take off. One researcher put Spirit in the cage, covered the top, and went to the control room, where, with a second investigator, he watched the timing clocks. After three minutes the first researcher removed the cat from the cage. There was a rest period; then three more tests were made. Twenty-eight tests were conducted, four each day for seven days.

All concerned knew the purpose of this series of directional experiments except the kitten. At least, no evidence has been offered to suggest that Spirit understood English or read minds. During the first four days the kitten had been active inside the cage. After that, Spirit stayed where it had been placed, seldom touching another wedge. As a whole, the tests were not statistically significant.

"If we look only at the four trials on which the kitten was active," the investigators wrote later, "we find an indication of orientation toward Harary's OB (out-of-body) position." Dr. Morris, Harary, Joseph Janis, and John Hartwell expressed this opinion in "Studies of Communications During Out-of-Body Experiences," published in the January 1978 issue of the *Journal of the American Society for Psychical Research.*

By the time new experiments were conducted in 1974 to determine whether Spirit could detect both the direction and the distance from which Harary's invisible presence would be manifested, the kitten had matured; Spirit had become a cat.

For these tests a target area seven feet high, ten feet long and ten feet wide was selected at Duke University. Strips of tape divided the floor into four quarters. A television camera aimed at a tilted convex mirror enabled an observer in another chamber to have an unobstructed view of the floor on the screen of a monitor. Blue, relaxing at the Psychical Research Foundation, was to send his inner self along the same ethereal route usually taken—but in the reverse direction.

In an investigation of this sort it is essential for the cat to be in a central position on the floor of the target room. If carried there by an experimenter, the animal might follow the experimenter to the door. A restraining device was rigged to keep the cat in place before each test began. Spirit was covered by an opaque container. A rope ran from the top over a pulley and out of the room. A pull on the far end of the rope lifted the cover and released the cat.

An experimenter, John Hartwell, watched Spirit's actions on the monitor and charted the cat's movements on a piece of paper. After three sessions and twelve tests "no consistent relationship" was found between Spirit's movements and the randomly selected target sites for Blue's consciousness.

Though the cat was not aware of Blue's arrivals, Hartwell apparently was. Four times he jotted down the hour and the minute when he sensed Blue's presence. All were within out-of-the body projection times. Hartwell once noted that he saw Blue's likeness in a corner of the target room via the monitor. Later it was learned that this was the area that Harary was supposed to be visiting. Unfortunately, the test had not been videotaped.

This sighting and one made by Jerry Posner, a volunteer aide during early alphabet tests, gave rise to rumors that doppelgängers—spirit doubles—had been seen at the foundation. Posner said that Blue's face had floated above the letter *r*. Posner seems to have seen the phantom face more clearly than Blue did the *r;* he called it a *k*.

According to the report in the January 1978 *Journal* previously cited, "Persons designated as detectors did poorly during the four-period procedure." Those assigned to equipment fared better, notably Hartwell while monitoring the third series of experiments with the cat.

Various instruments were employed in efforts to establish that Harary's consciousness had visited a target site, among them devices that measured fields of electromagnetism and temperature variations. The readings were inconsistent with the lengths and times of out-of-body excursions. Little resemblance was found between psychophysiological data gathered while Blue was alleged to be away from his body and while he was dreaming.

The out-of-the-body experiments made by the Psychical Research Foundation in Durham, like those of the American Society for Psychical Research, did not produce proof that these alleged projections were experienced by the living, and, as no tests were made with the critically ill, the paramount issue—does a soul leave the body at death?—remained unresolved.

11.

Into the Brightness

The largest project funded by the Kidd legacy—a survey of deathbed visions in India—enabled Dr. Karlis Osis, research director of the American Society for Psychical Research, to compare the concepts of another culture with those he had gathered and analyzed in the United States. His interest in parapsychology went back some forty years. Born in 1917 about thirty miles from Riga, Latvia, Karlis, at the age of fifteen, suddenly became elated when an aunt died in another room of the family farmhouse. There was no reason for him to be happy, but the room seemed to be brighter and a buoyant euphoria surged through his body. He wondered later whether the aunt's joy on being released from her pain had somehow been transmitted to him.

A dissertation on "The Hypothesis of Extrasensory Perception" earned him a doctorate in psychology at the University of Munich in 1950. As a research associate in Dr. J. B. Rhine's Parapsychology Laboratory at Duke University, he tested, among other things, the receptivity of cats to unspoken thoughts. His work at Duke prepared him for the post of research director at the Parapsychology Foundation in Manhattan. There he tested mediums, probed poltergeist disturbances, and, inspired by Sir William Barrett's *Death-bed Visions*

(1926) outlined a comprehensive plan to make a census of a phase of psychic phenomena never systematically studied previously.

Barrett's book had been written after the physicist's wife, a surgeon, told him about a woman who had died following childbirth. The dying woman described a luminous world and phantom people that only she could see. She smiled as she recognized her dead father and sister and regretted that her husband and the newborn child could not go with her into "the lovely brightness."

Dr. Barrett, a founder of the Society for Psychical Research, had read about similar visions. One element in his wife's story particularly intrigued him. The patient had not been told that her sister had died. How had she known? This and similar accounts related by Dr. Barrett made a strong impression on Dr. Osis.

An earlier volume, Dr. James H. Hyslop's *Psychical Research and the Resurrection* (1908), had explored this area in a chapter titled "Visions of the Dying." Dr. Hyslop, a former Columbia University professor of ethics and logic, was then the dominant figure of the American Society for Psychical Research. He noted that "the alleged visions which many dying persons are said to have had of friends who have passed away before them" were "well worthy of a most searching investigation." These statements "might easily be collected and made the subject of statistical study and psychological analysis." This is what Dr. Osis hoped to do.

Dr. Hyslop cited a letter he had received. A boy of nine regained consciousness following an operation for peritonitis and, before he died, engaged in the following conversation:

"Mother, dear, don't you see little sister over there?"

"No, where is she?"

"Right over there. She is looking at me. . . . There comes Mrs. C——(a lady of whom he was very fond who had died two years before) and she is smiling just as she used to. She is smiling and wants me to come. There is Roy! I am going to them. I don't want to leave you, but you'll come to me soon, won't you? Open the door and let them in. They are waiting for me outside."

The letter also reported that the boy had seen his grandmother. The boy's mother verified this account for Dr. Hyslop. She said that the sister's death had occurred before his birth and that he had never met this grandmother. Roy, one of the boy's friends, had died a year or so before the operation.

Two people, identified as reliable persons, dictated another account in Dr. Hyslop's presence. About a month before a boy's death of cancer, a medium had told his mother that Bright Eyes, a spirit guide, would visit the child. The guide apparently manifested the night previous to his death, for the boy said a small girl appeared near the bed and he did not know her. Several minutes before his death his nurse heard him say, "I think they are taking me."

Later, through the medium, the boy said that he had been lifted out of his body. Pain ceased as he left the flesh. He had an urge to return to the body, but he was in a cloud. He had been delighted by the sensation of being raised by unseen hands into the rarified atmosphere. He could see his dead father in the distance.

Searching for other stories of this sort, Dr. Hyslop found one in *Psychics: Facts and Theories* (1893), a book written by Dr. Minot J. Savage. A girl named Edith, dying of diptheria in June 1889, had not been told that her young playmate Jennie had died a few days earlier. Edith approached her final hour calmly. She said she saw several of her friends who had died. Then, in surprise she called to her father, "Why, papa, I am going to take Jennie with me. Why, papa! Why, papa! You did not tell me that Jennie was here! Extending her arms as if to welcome the unseen playmate, she added, "O, Jennie, I'm so glad you are here."

There were twenty-two incidents in an article Professor Ernesto Bozzano, an eminent Italian investigator of psychical phenomena, prepared for *Annals of Psychical Science,* the English edition of a French periodical. One was from a biography of the Reverend Dwight L. Moody, a famous American evangelist. His son recalled that before Moody died, he said, "Earth recedes, heaven opens up before me. I have been beyond the gates. God is calling. Don't call me back. It is beautiful. If this is death it is sweet." With a radiant face and joyous words, Moody called, "Dwight! Irene! I see the children's faces." (Two of Moody's grandchildren had died earlier).

Another of Professor Bozzano's examples had appeared in Alfred Smedley's *Some Reminiscences* (1900). Smedley's dying wife saw forms in the room that were not visible to him. "Why! There is sister Charlotte here; and mother and father and brother John and sister Mary! And now they have brought Bessie Heap! They are all here. O! how beautiful." She expressed disappointment that her husband could not see the family and Bessie Heap, the reliable nurse who had once looked after her.

Dr. Hyslop quoted from a letter that Dr. Paul Edwards had sent to *Light,* a British weekly, in April 1900. A woman dying of consumption in a small California town told her husband that she suffered no pain, so he should not sob. She had loved him in this life and would continue to do so in the next. Before she made the transition, she said, "I see people moving—all in white. The music is strangely enchanting—Oh! there is Sadie; she is with me—and she knows who I am." The husband exclaimed, "Sissy! you are out of your mind." The wife answered, "Oh, dear! why did you call me here again? Now it will be hard for me to go away again; I was so pleased while there—it was so delightful—so soothing. . . . I am going away again and will not come back to you even if you call me."

The physician at the deathbed of James Moore, a tenor, heard the singer's last words, Dr. Hyslop reported. "There is mother! Why, mother, have you come here to see me? No, no, I'm coming to see *you.* Just wait, mother, I'm almost over. I can jump it. Wait, mother."

After citing several cases published by the Society for Psychical Research, Dr. Hyslop wrote, "We may ultimately induce physicians in the hospitals to instruct nurses and officers to make observations and to record all experiences of an hallucinatory character or otherwise." Dr. Hyslop thought that such cases would be rare, but that this approach would give "a scientific character" to an investigation.

Half a century later, when Dr. Osis planned his study, he realized that it would be impractical to get the data he needed in the way Hyslop had suggested. Even if enough hospitals cooperated to make the survey sufficiently large to be statistically impressive, it might take years before a sizable number of relevant cases accumulated.

There was an alternative way to get the necessary material for analysis, and this was the one he proposed to employ if Eileen Garrett, the president of the Parapsychology Foundation, and former Congresswoman Frances P. Bolton, whose money had made previous grants possible, approved of his plan. A noted medium herself, as well as an able editor, publisher, and administrator, Mrs. Garrett had crusaded for a more scientific attitude toward psychic phenomena; Mrs. Bolton, who had talked to her dead husband through a Garrett spirit guide, shared this zeal. They gave the project their blessings, and the funds required to carry it out.

Near the end of 1959 Dr. Osis sent a two-page questionnaire to ten thousand American physicians and nurses. This "stratified random sample" encompassed three thousand doctors who were at hospitals as staff members, residents, or interns; two thousand physicians with private practices; and five thousand nurses. Recipients were asked to estimate how many terminally ill patients they had treated, how many times they had been present at the time of death, and how often patients had had hallucinations. Were there people involved in these hallucinations? Were the people alive, dead, religious or fantasy figures, or unidentifiable? Were patients elated just before they died?

Like many people who are annoyed by surveys of any sort, 9,360 recipients tossed the questionnaire into the closest wastebasket. Responses came from 640. From the estimated number of hallucinations recollected and reported, Dr. Osis somehow arrived at very precise statistics: 1,318 patients had seen apparitions of people, 884 had had scenic visions, and 753 had seemed to be more blissful as they died.

More detailed queries were mailed to 160 of the 640 respondents, or they were questioned at greater length by telephone. A report on the survey, *Deathbed Observations by Physicians and Nurses,* was published by the Parapsychology Foundation in 1961. The following year Dr. Osis became research director of the American Society for Psychical Research.

The man who would finance the second phase of Osis's study, Chester F. Carlson, inventor of the Xerox process, loomed large on the parapsychology front, though his behind-the-scenes activities were not publicized. About 1950 his wife Dorris began hearing words that sometimes presaged events; on occasion she visualized scenes. Once, for example, the word lilliput came to her mind. She wrote it down, sure that it was in some way significant. Less than two months later she accompanied her husband on a trip to Canada. While he checked in at a Toronto hotel, she glanced at the magazines on display at a shop in the lobby. One was a British publication that she had never seen before. Its name was *Lilliput.* Turning the pages, she found an article about two people who had shared identical dreams.

Carlson, she said later, had listened to her stories about these strange occurences, but she did not realize that they had impressed him until he started to experiment in this area himself. Relaxing one night in an easy chair adjacent to the fireplace, he shut his eyes, as he often did when mulling over technical snags that developed during his work. On the far side of the room she sat on a sofa, her thoughts on the words she was reading. A cocker spaniel dozed on the rug. Suddenly a loud noise, like the bursting of an air-filled paper bag brought her to her feet and woke the dog. Carlson admitted that he had been testing his own psychic powers. He had tried for more than fifteen minutes to hear one of the voices that she had told him about. He was ready to turn his attention to other matters when the percussive sound startled him. It seemed to come from the center of the room, midway between floor and ceiling.

That experience, for which her husband could find no rational explanation, marked, Dorris Carlson recalled, the beginning of his serious consideration of psychical phenomena. By the time he met Dr. Osis he had read many books on the subject and was willing to give both moral and monetary support to carefully planned scientific projects.

Dr. Osis, spurred on by the reception that his monograph on deathbed visions had received in parapsychology circles, designed another survey to validate his findings. Like the first it would be expensive. Carlson studied the proposal, asked several penetrating questions, and told Dr. Osis to proceed.

The second census centered on doctors and nurses in New York, Connecticut, New Jersey, Pennsylvania, and Rhode Island. Though only five thousand—half as many as in the original project—received questionnaires, the response was far greater. There were one thousand and four replies.

A preliminary study indicated that the results confirmed the original data. Wondering whether the religious and cultural beliefs of patients in another country would be reflected in the apparitions that they described before dying, Dr. Osis sought sponsorship for an overseas survey. He discussed this aspect of the study with Dr. Gardner Murphy, who was then president of the American Society for Psychical Research. Dr. Murphy thought that Japan would be an ideal country to probe, as the pattern of life there was strikingly different. However, Chester Carlson opted for India; he and his wife had been experimenting with yoga meditations. As he was to pay for the venture, his view prevailed. Before the project could get under way, an unforeseen circumstance brought it to an abrupt halt. Chester F. Carlson, founder of one of the most successful American business enterprises, the Xerox Corporation, and princely patron of psychical research, died at the age of sixty on September 19, 1968.

Two months later the benefactor whose contributions to

the society had been made anonymously was honored at an American Society for Psychical Research Lecture Forum. The May 1969 issue of the society's *Proceedings* carried the speeches made by his widow, Dr. Gardner Murphy, two trustees—Dr. Gertrude R. Schmeidler and Dr. Ian Stevenson—and Dr. Osis, the director of research. Dr. Osis expressed his gratitude to the modest man who had helped in so many ways with various projects. "He permitted no honors to come to him but it was his hand that cultivated most of the best psychical research projects of the 1960's."

The third and final phase of the deathbed-vision investigations did not begin until the American Society for Psychical Research had been awarded the $270,000 legacy of James Kidd. Dr. Osis reported in the Autumn 1973 issue of the *ASPR Newsletter* that he and Dr. Erlendur Haraldsson, a parapsychologist who lived in Iceland, had made two information-seeking expeditions to India. Questionnaires answered by 704 physicians and nurses there had been read. About half contained relevant data. Interviews with this portion of the respondents followed.

Apparitions had been seen by 255 dying patients; 64 who recovered from a crisis condition also saw images of humans. Glimpses of the afterworld were described by another 48. In 68 instances those who died appeared to be calmer just before they expired. In India, as in the United States, patients whose mental faculties were either in good condition or only slightly affected saw more apparitions than those who experienced deliria. By a two-to-one ratio sufferers with diseased brains, however, saw more apparitions of the living than of the dead.

Most hallucinating American patients believed that the spectral forms had come to escort them to the world beyond. An even larger number of Indian patients, seventy-five percent, also thought this the reason that the apparitions had appeared. The vast majority of American patients indicated that the transition was painless; they did not fight to resist it. A third of the Indians felt that strong efforts were being made to wrench away their inner selves; they struggled to prevent this violent separation.

The most important issue of the survival problem, Dr. Osis stressed, was whether the apparitions seen by the dying were simply hallucinations or something more tangible. He considered this issue at greater length in "What Did the Dying See?" in the *ASPR Newsletter* of Winter 1975.

There were, by his definition, two sorts of hallucinations—"Disneyland" and "mountain." The former were described by those who had them in aimless sentences and were related to incidents that had occurred earlier in their lives. The latter referred to the afterworld. He gave an example cited by a physician. A woman of sixty, dying from a painful cancer of the intestines, suddenly called out the name of her dead husband, smiled, and said that she was going to him.

Current studies of dream and sleep states and fantasies induced by narcotics had shown that visions included symbolic representations of emotional maladjustments, fears, and aspirations, as well as remembered incidents. Stating that ESP was a known source of images in hallucinations, Dr. Osis pondered whether ESP enabled the dying to have a preview of the afterlife. A physician recounted a deathbed experience in which a woman patient told him that his grandfather, whom she had known, was standing at his side and that he should return home immediately. There he learned that his grandfather had died suddenly thirty minutes earlier.

In the first American survey more than three-quarters of those who died less than ten minutes after telling about an apparition identified the specter as someone who had come to lead them to another world. Even more, over eighty-five percent, fell into this category in the second American sample. Only the Indians who struggled to stay in their bodies during their final ten minutes made similar identifications.

At the Hour of Death (1977), a book by Dr. Osis and Dr. Haraldsson, presented an analysis of the three studies and told of some of the difficulties that they had had in India. Advised not to mail out questionnaires because the postal service was slow and unreliable and finding that telephone calls were rarely put through without a long delay, the researchers decided to limit their quest for data to personal interviews in a single state, Uttar Pradesh. They traveled from Delhi to Meerut, Agra, Allahabad, Kanpur, Aligarh, Farrukhabad, and Benares. Most of the interviews were conducted in university hospitals. They explained their mission to an assembled staff; then the listeners were given copies of the questionnaire and asked to answer the queries. After the papers had been collected and sorted, personal interviews were scheduled. While the majority of the physicians spoke English, many of the nurses did not, so an interpreter translated their replies.

The researchers learned that older Indians on their deathbeds expressed religious feelings twice as frequently as those who were younger. This ratio was reversed in America. While Americans saw religious figures in the afterlife, Indians glimpsed them in their hospital rooms. Curiously, more female apparitions were sighted by Indians and a larger number of male specters by Americans. Though a Grim Reaper figure was not reported by any American, several Indians said that Yama, the symbol of death, or his assistants, the Yamdoots, had come to take them away.

There were many visions of heaven in the transcultural study, but only one of hell, reported by a Rhode Island woman who had been born in Italy. The most often noted features of heaven were gates and gardens. One American patient said that a taxi had taken her to the gates of a heavenly garden. Others likened heaven to a lovely sunset, a bright golden glow, and a beautifully furnished room. An Indian woman described it as mountains topped by snow.

Some of the dying Americans heard music. Sometimes the music was played on a heavenly organ, sung by a choir, or by angels. An American woman in her late sixties did not see the hereafter but had a vision of Confederate soldiers wearing gray Civil War uniforms and armed with rifles, standing guard around her bed. Surprisingly few of those approaching death saw God, though a dying patient who recovered said that he had talked with him. God told the man that he had arrived too soon and turned him away.

Dr. Osis and Dr. Haraldsson admitted in their book that they had been critical of the survival hypothesis before making the survey. At its completion they were both more inclined to accept it.

Two years before this study was set in type the last of the Kidd legacy was spent. The final portion, Dr. Osis revealed in the Summer 1975 issue of the *ASPR Newsletter,* paid for another journey to India by Dr. Haraldsson and himself. They had heard wondrous stories on previous visits about "outstanding swamis" who could project images of themselves from their bodies. Many people claimed to have seen these doubles, which appeared to be solid, talked, wore clothes, and sometimes left solid objects as mementos for onlookers before disappearing.

During this ten-week trip the parapsychologists centered their observations on two alleged avatars, men reputed to have godlike powers, including that of astral projection. The investigators traveled across India seeking eye-witness accounts of the projections of Sathya Sai Baba and Dadaji. Some witnesses understood and spoke English. Interpreters were required for those who testified in Bengali, Hindi, Telugu, Kannada, Tamil, Gujarati, and Malayalam.

Eight people vouched for the tale that Sai Baba had been in one part of the country in double form, while others attested that he had been seen in his body about three hundred miles away. The investigators had the privilege of eleven close-up sessions with Sai Baba in his ashram. The swami, who has spent most of his years in Puttaparthi, a town north of Bangalore, is a clean-shaven man with a mass of bushy dark hair. His followers in India and abroad are said to be in the millions. He wears a long, slip-over garment with sleeves extending to his wrists. Hundreds wait to see him each day, hoping to be chosen for the two small groups that he selects for private meeting as he strolls in a wide path cleared for him through the crowd. Foreigners, especially those who do not appear to be hippies, have a better chance of being singled out than the poor devotees who sometimes stand for days without receiving as much as a nod.

Sai Baba amazed the psychic researchers with "inexplicable" feats during which small objects appeared, disappeared, or changed into others. "At no time," Dr. Osis wrote, "did we see anything that suggested trickery." More than fifty cassettes filled with data were recorded during their stay. These would be transcribed and studied. "In fact," Dr. Osis wrote, "the top swamis seem to offer a great deal from which the West can learn—by carefully applying the rigors of the scientific method."

As a professional magician, the present writer has traveled in seventy-two countries, including India. I too have searched for occult wonders there, but without success. I read with the greatest interest the Haraldsson-Osis report "The Appearance and Disappearance of Objects in the Presence of Sri Sathya Sai Baba" in the January 1977 issue of the *Journal of the American Society for Psychical Research.* The size of the objects had not been specified in the title. Would small Indian boys climb suspended ropes and disappear? Or elephants materialize from nowhere? Neither. The objects were of a size that could be held in the hand.

The parapsychologists saw more than twenty demonstrations of this sort. Sai Baba seemingly materialized vibuti (sacred ashes) with a wave of his hand. With another wave he produced a hundred-dollar gold ring, which he casually presented to Dr. Osis as a memento. Then a double rudraksha, which looked and felt like two naturally joined acorns, appeared. After it had been passed for examination and returned, Sai Baba held it between his hands, blew on them, and converted the unadorned rudraksha into one decorated with small gold shields and tiny rubies. This eighty-dollar trinket he gave to Dr. Haraldsson.

These and other feats described in the text have been exhibited by other "holy men" in India—and by conjurers! I have seen the first trick in a movie on Sai Baba, where he is pictured thrusting his arm up into an inverted cannister, to convey the impression that it is empty, and then producing a flow of sacred ashes from the interior. The cannister is a standard piece of magical apparatus. I could teach a six-year-old boy how to do this in a few minutes.

Sai Baba's sleight-of-hand is another matter. With his years of practice, he presents this beautifully and seemingly effortlessly. Of course intelligent laypeople are fooled; that is the purpose of magic. Anyone thoroughly familiar with the principles of legerdemain can follow move for move how the ash is produced. The parapsychologists should have been alerted when Sai Baba refused to allow them to test him, that is, to do the feats under controlled conditions. It is strange that experienced investigators of alleged phenomena would travel halfway around the world and suggest that such hanky-panky hocus-pocus was "paranormal," without having had an expert magician on the site as an observer.

Oh yes—about that legendary self-projection feat of the great avatars that the parapsychologists had flown to India to document—they never saw it.

A story appeared in the June 16, 1975, issue of the *New York Times,* on a page with several obituaries, reporting that the American Society for Psychical Research had filed documents with the Probate Court of Phoenix, Arizona, according to which "it did not accomplish its goal of proving the existence of a human soul."

12.

Life after Life

$\mathbf{D}$r. Raymond A. Moody, Jr., the author of *Life After Life*, gathered accounts of near-death experiences because they intrigued him. He had never been on the border between life and death himself and knew little about psychic research and even less about thanatology—the study of death and the dying. Born in Georgia in 1945, he received his Ph.D. in philosophy at the University of Virginia. After teaching a few years in North Carolina, he returned to get a medical degree. He planned to study psychiatry and eventually to teach a course on the philosophy of medicine.

While still an undergraduate, Moody had heard a professor of psychiatry at the School of Medicine tell about two times, several minutes apart, when he had been clinically dead. During one of these periods the professor felt that he had left his body, that his consciousness had been detached. When the professor repeated the story on another occasion, Moody taped it. Later one of Dr. Moody's students told a similar story about a grandmother who had almost died. Other students reported almost parallel incidents.

When Dr. Moody spoke about these incidents during the talks he gave for various organizations, more people added to his collection of data. By the time he had classified one hundred and fifty cases and interviewed fifty survivors, he had enough information for a book. His 1975 book on the recollections of survivors from the moment their hearts stopped until they regained consciousness became a best seller, and for a very good reason. His viewpoint was that of the average person. Amazed that people had these experiences, he was not sure what to make of them.

To illustrate the range of the reported phenomena, Dr. Moody presented a composite case. An apparently dying man, at the height of his agony, is aware that the physician has pronounced him dead. He hears a persistent noise as his consciousness speeds through a black cylindrical opening. Emerging from the far side, he looks down as efforts are being made to revive his body. Other spirit entities greet him. He recognizes dead members of his family, relatives, and friends. A glowing being radiating love is present as scenes of the dying man's past flash before him. However, he cannot enter the realm of eternal life; his cycle of existence on earth has not been completed. With great reluctance he leaves this sphere of happiness and tranquillity and returns to his body.

No one, Dr. Moody stressed, had experienced all of these elements, but almost everyone interviewed had experienced at least one of them. Some who had nearly died did not remember anything after they regained consciousness.

A woman with a liver ailment, who was allergic to many drugs and whose heart had stopped, recalled that she had heard a radiologist telephone her doctor and tell him, "I've killed your patient." She also said that she had heard the conversation in the room before being revived and had not felt any pain or sensation when needles were inserted into her temporarily lifeless body.

Descriptions of the cessation of pain, collected by Dr. Moody, were consistent with the feelings of peacefulness noted by others. The sounds heard ranged from ringing and buzzing noises to soothing music. Souls sped through dark areas on their way to outer freedom—caverns, valleys, voids, tunnels—even sewers. The common theme was that the passageways were long and cylindrical.

Many, but not all, consciousness separations had been experienced in hospitals. One woman said that she had left her body while nearly drowning in a swimming pool. A young man's consciousness had been separated when the car he was driving crashed into another.

The majority said that it was difficult to describe the spirit forms that they had assumed. These ethereal "bodies" could see, but not move, the objects they touched. While they could not turn a doorknob or push open a swinging door, it was not necessary to do so, as their spirits could pass directly through wood and other solid materials.

Some survivors said that they heard living people talking in hospital rooms; others knew what was being said without actually hearing the words. It was very lonely being in a room with the living. There was no way to communicate with them or touch them to let them know an invisible entity was present.

Occasionally other spirits were seen. A woman who almost died while giving birth saw her grandmother and a former classmate, along with other departed friends, near the ceiling. Old friends who had died sometimes came to visit. Long before his near-death crisis, one man frequently saw the spirit of another, who had been killed weeks before. After the crisis had passed, this visitor no longer came to the hospital room. Those who said that they saw luminous strangers identified them as divine beings or angels.

Recalling incidents of her past life which she had seen while out of her body, a woman viewed herself as a child near a creek, as a child with her sister, as a child crying because a toy had been broken, then as a Girl Scout and as a student in high school and college. These flashing visions were in color and seemed to be as real as they had been when the events occurred.

The approach to eternity varied. One person remembered being on a ship that never reached a distant port. Another saw a land with houses and people in a golden atmosphere but could not cross the boundary to reach this haven. Still another's way was blocked by a magnificent closed door.

Those who had near-death experiences and recovered to tell about them lost their fears of dying. They *knew* that a more beautiful world was in the offing, not an end of consciousness and oblivion.

None of the near-death survivors interviewed by Dr. Moody described hell, though a man who had tried to kill himself after his wife died said that he had visited the region briefly. He saw enough to make him regret the suicide attempt; he did not recall the scenery.

Though Dr. Moody is a Methodist and a philosopher, he did not reveal how the study had affected his thinking. Nor did he discuss his personal reactions on television and radio talk-shows, or when interviewed by the press. Questioned by students of psychic phenomena and newspaper reporters, he answered calmly that he was not a crusader and had not made a scientific survey. What he had imagined to be a rare phenomenon when he began his work now seemed to have been experienced by many people.

Glancing around the city room of the Chicago *Sun-Times,* where more than seventy men and women were at work, he told reporter Jane Gregory in November 1976, "It would be my guess that there is at least one in this room who has had the 'life after life' experience." Then with typical caution he added, "If not in this room, certainly in this building."

Dr. Moody had not mentioned the names of the people whom he had interviewed. Several, however, volunteered to appear with him on television. Others gave more details of their visions to enterprising reporters. Danion Brinkley, a twenty-seven-year-old North Carolinian, said in the March 27, 1977, issue of the Washington *Post* that a bolt of lightning had struck him as he made a phone call. The force of the bolt had thrown him across the room. His wife rushed him to a hospital, where artificial respiration kept him alive. Once, when pain had numbed his senses, he had seen a glowing presence in "a place that was blue and gray, calm and peaceful." There, Brinkley recalled, every emotion he had ever felt was re-experienced "simultaneously." After regaining consciousness, he had difficulty in describing this assault on his senses.

Attacks by ministers and physicians on Dr. Moody's research were not as severe as he had expected. Some clergymen found the study helpful in their work with the dying. A Methodist minister admitted that it had strengthened his faith, though he thought that without this faith the reported incidents would not have swayed his opinion. A few clergymen charged Dr. Moody with practicing satanism. An Episcopalian advised the author to spend more time trying to right the wrongs of this life than attempting to gain an insight into the next.

Critical physicians held that the near-death visions could have been induced by anesthetics or drugs. Following operations where ether had been administered, patients had remembered entering a long dark tunnel of the sort recalled by Dr. Moody's sources. Psychological and neurological disturbances also produced hallucinations.

Dr. Moody had more than three hundred cases in his files when *Reflections on Life After Life* was published in 1977. To the basic elements of his composite near-death experience, he now could add several more: Some people had suddenly acquired a complete knowledge of the universe (unfortunately they did not retain it upon being resuscitated); others had sighted the traditional heaven; a few had visited an area between this existence and the next.

Commenting on the fact that more stories of near-death experiences were being reported now than in the past, Dr. Moody said that fewer patients had been revived then. Primitive methods of resuscitation were not as effective. Years ago, heat had been applied to abdomens, and seemingly lifeless bodies had been flogged in attempts to revive them.

Paracelsus, a physician who practiced in Switzerland in the sixteenth century, puffed air into the lungs of inert clients by inserting bellows into their mouths. Elsewhere in Europe people who had stopped breathing were sometimes draped face down over barrels and rolled back and forth. Others were fastened in a similar position across the backs of horses. Bouncing up and down as the horses trotted, the patients sometimes revived. Medicine men in North America employed a reverse procedure. Rectal instruments akin to syringes shot smoke into the bodies of near-dead Indians. (Adrenalin was not used as a heart stimulant until the early years of this century.)

Dr. Moody had been asked whether he had considered hypnotic regression as a way to produce more information about near-death experiences. He had, but after consulting with a medical hypnotist and learning that a subject might suffer the agonies of approaching death, he had abandoned the project. Since then, he had heard that during a similar regression experiment the subject had had to be revived after cardiac arrest.

Dr. Moody had not expressed his personal opinion about the near-death examples set forth in his first book. In his second he wrote that as a Methodist he accepted the doctrine of survival past the grave and that he believed in the incidents reported to him as "manifestations" of the afterlife.

Life After Life offered data collected by a philosopher-psychiatrist who had been puzzled by stories of near-death experiences. It had not been written to convince readers that souls survive or to affirm a religious belief. Few books are so impartial. For example, the announced purpose of Jess E. Weiss's *The Vestibule* (1972) was "to establish with more certainty that there is an afterlife. Thereby alleviating the sting of death." The author, a World War II veteran, had been severely wounded by shrapnel while serving with the First Infantry Division in Germany. After three operations Weiss's right hand and arm were paralyzed, and his right leg was shorter by two inches. In desperation he went to a Christian Science practitioner. The curative measures were painful, but he regained the use of his right arm and learned how to walk without a special shoe.

Inspired to prepare others for the entry into another, better life, Weiss assembled accounts of those who, like himself, had triumphed over adversity and the fear of dying. One, the Reverend Burris Jenkins, had been an atheist until a near-death experience changed the course of his life.

In August 1957 an accidental explosion blasted Jenkins up through the timbers of his cruiser in Cold Spring Harbor, New York. Falling back close to the engine, he saw gas spurting from a damaged pipe and, though badly burned, made it to the dock. Firemen drove him to Huntington Hospital; then, after emergency medication, he was rushed to Roosevelt Hospital in New York City. For more than four hours a team of physicians peeled charred tissue from his body.

Several days later, as Jenkins stared at a television commercial in his hospital room, he became aware that he had left his body and was floating backwards over the bed. He went out through a window backwards and soared high over the city into the clouds. Alone in a region far past the galaxy, with his speed constantly increasing, he was engulfed by a feeling of desolation. The isolation frightened him; then he sensed presences near him, other disembodied entities like himself, and saw the light that is the source of life. He realized that he would not be one of the happy spirits existing harmoniously with the light and cried out, "God help me!" Instantly he was back in the hospital room. The television was still on, but the commercial had ended. After he left the hospital and became a pilot for the Navy, this flight to another world stayed in Jenkins's mind. At the age of thirty-seven he retired from the service and entered the ministry.

Another of Weiss's cases was that of Dr. George G. Ritchie, Jr., who had a near-death experience while a private at Camp Barkeley in Texas. Doctors were urgently needed for combat duty, and Ritchie had qualified for special training at a medical school in Richmond, Virginia. Hospitalized for what seemed to him a minor ailment—a cold in his chest—he developed a high fever. While standing in front of an X-ray machine, he collapsed. Awaking in an unfamiliar room, he remembered that he had to go to Richmond. He looked for his uniform but was unable to find it. He noticed that a dead man was in the bed, wearing a fraternity ring exactly like his. He sped out of the room and down the corridor to the front door of the building. Along the way he ran *through* someone coming in his direction.

Out in the night air Ritchie forgot about the train and began to fly. Doubts assailed him. Would the medical school admit an invisible student? Would they know he was there? He swooped down to a telephone pole and passed his hand through a wire. The solid wire had not stopped it. He realized that the body on the bed must be his own. Changing destinations, he headed back to the hospital, arriving at almost the same moment that the thought entered his mind. He went from room to room. There were many sleeping soldiers; none was dead. Finally he found the room and the corpse with his ring on the finger.

The corpse had been covered. Ritchie reached out to take the covering from the face, but his hand passed through the material. He was unable to grasp it. Then a new problem worried him: How could he get back into his body? He was dead.

The room began to glow. The light was brighter than any he had ever seen. He knew that the light was Christ, and his fears were replaced by an exuberant feeling of happiness. Scenes from his past flooded the room. Everything he had ever done was visible to him. He saw himself at home with his family, as a student in school, running with members of his track team. He was conscious that the presence in the room was asking him what he had done during his brief span on earth and whether he had told others about Christ. When he began to make apologies, he was transported to another world, a dim world filled with self-centered people. Their faces were glum; they were despondent.

The light grew brighter, and another world came into focus. People here were on a higher level. They carved statues, pondered the meaning of life, composed music, and invented worthwhile devices. They studied, surrounded by great books, and listened to eloquent teachers. Far in the distance was a gleaming city of light. The buildings glowed and so did the inhabitants, as brightly as the light that filled the small room in the Texas hospital. Then the light faded, and Ritchie fell into a troubled sleep. When he opened his eyes, he was back in his body and on a bed.

The attending physician said later that Ritchie had been clinically dead. Nine minutes after his heart had stopped, a soldier noticed a slight movement that sent him racing to the doctor. An injection of adrenalin revived the heart. Two of Dr. George G. Ritchie's most valued possessions are affidavits signed by the doctor and a nurse saying that he died of double lobar pneumonia on December 20, 1943.

Adrenalin also reactivated a motionless heart in a second case cited in Weiss's *The Vestibule.* As an intern at Pennsylvania Hospital in Philadelphia, Dr. Martin C. Sampson had seen the condition of a man, who was approaching the age of fifty, deteriorate. Day after day when Dr. Sampson came to the patient's bedside, there was no sign of improvement. The man had suffered from rheumatic fever as a boy, and the hardening of his arteries with advancing years had increased the strain on his heart. Oxygen was pumped into the tent covering his body to keep him alive.

Early one summer evening Dr. Sampson responded to a call from a nurse. The patient was sinking fast. Medications brought him only slight relief. He managed to whisper that his family should be called. Minutes later his heart stopped beating.

Dr. Sampson shoved the oxygen tent aside and began giving the man artifical respiration. Pausing only to inject adrenalin, he continued the manual pressure. The resident physician came into the ward. He considered it futile to attempt to reactivate a heart as damaged as this one and went to telephone the patient's wife. Undeterred, Dr. Sampson pushed, relaxed, pushed, relaxed. Finally the patient started breathing again. When his wife arrived, he could talk. He told her that their love would continue in the afterlife. She expressed her belief that they would never be parted.

Dr. Sampson, marveling at this recovery, asked the patient

what he recalled of the period of unconsciousness. The man told him that his pain had ceased and that he had heard soothing music. He had been with God. The music had faded when he opened his eyes and saw the doctor. He had not been dreaming, he added emphatically. He died several hours later.

Reports of an afterlife differ in detail, but usually mirror the thoughts of others who claim to have been there. The dying man in Philadelphia was sure that he and his wife would be together eternally. Mothers have visions of happy spirit children.

Julia Phillips Ruopp, a clergyman's wife, lived many years after her vision of the afterworld. She recalled the experience, which she had had thirty years earlier, in the magazine *Guideposts* in 1963. During an operation for a thyroid condition she heard a nurse say that her pulse was gradually getting fainter. She opened her eyes. She was above her body, looking down. She entered a dark corridor and without fear went through it until she reached an area of pulsating light. Peering through a gigantic convex surface, similar to one half of a huge transparent ball, she saw singing children at play in an orchard. Red apples were hanging on the trees. The colors were brilliant; the air was clear.

Weightless and feeling a divine presence near her, she knew that she could go through the enormous window, but something held her back. She shut her eyes tightly. The blackness swept her again into the corridor. She descended through it and into her body, slipping into the head. When she moved one of her fingers, she heard the nurse say, "Glory be; she's coming to. It's been fifteen minutes."

In the May 1971 issue of the Canadian Medical Association *Journal* Dr. R. L. MacMillan and Dr. E. W. G. Brown reported a sixty-eight-year-old man's memories of his sensations following cardiac arrest. He had been lying face up in an intensive care unit. Tubes inserted in his body and wires running to a polygraph limited his movements. He recalled heaving a sigh, and then thinking that he was falling asleep when his head fell to one side. Suddenly he saw his body from the waist up, as it would appear if reflected in a mirror. An inner body ascended from it. This was not a vapor, though he could see his physical body through it. Once out, the inner self became slightly larger.

Then he was sitting on a small object as it carried him rapidly on a forty-five-degree course into the atmosphere above the earth. Alone in a drab bluish-gray sky, he saw a cloudlike formation below and to his left. It too was soaring at the speed of light and would collide with him unless he changed course. He quickly maneuvered and came down for a closer look at this menace. It was white, rectangular, and so full of holes that it reminded him of a sponge.

Avoiding this obstacle, he floated blissfully into a region of pale gold. Though he could not see the lower part of his body, he sensed that the ugly scars of a boyhood accident had been ripped away from his right leg as easily as adhesive tape is removed. "They have always said your body is made whole out here," he said to himself. While gliding serenely in the sky, he felt a heavy blow strike his left side. This did not hurt, but it disturbed his equilibrium. Another came, then another. He counted them. After the sixth he complained, "What the . . . are you doing?"

His eyes opened. He was in the intensive care unit. In reply to his questions, he learned that one of the nurses had been pounding him, trying to reactivate his heart. Later he thought that the golden atmosphere might have been a light centered on his eyes by a doctor making an examination. He had enjoyed the floating sensation so much that he told the doctor, "If I go out again, don't bring me back—it's so beautiful out there."

Religious beliefs are reflected in the descriptions that the devout give of the afterlife. Baptists are not apt to encounter Allah and Mohammed; they expect to see God and Jesus Christ. Marvin Ford, an Anaheim, California, mill foreman who led the gospel singing at Christian Center (later renamed Melodyland), testified that his consciousness popped from his body like a cork from a bottle when he stopped breathing at La Habra Community Hospital on January 1, 1972. He ascended to a city of light in the sky, a glowing metropolis with pearly gates, golden streets, and jasper walls. Jesus greeted him personally soon after his arrival.

Then, Ford said, the gold became transparent. Looking through it and through the equally transparent roof of the hospital where he had been, he saw the Reverend Dr. Ralph Wilkerson take the motionless hand of the body in the bed. The minister, speaking as a representative of Jesus on earth, commanded death to release its icy grip and permit the soul to reenter the flesh. Reluctant to leave heaven, Ford asked Jesus whether he could become a minister if he returned. Jesus commissioned him an officer in the forces of the Lord. Ford slipped back into the cold body on the bed, animated it, and smiled. A nurse fitted the plug of a machine that monitored heart beats into a socket. He heard the reassuring sounds which indicated that he was alive.

Ford's "Thirty Minutes in Heaven" appeared in the October 1976 issue of *Full Gospel Men's Voice.* In *Beyond and Back,* an inspirational book published the following year, Dr. Wilkerson wrote that Ford had had little formal education but that, as a result of this experience, he stirred and inspired those who heard him speak.

Dr. Wilkerson, an evangelical Baptist, himself attracts as many as twelve thousand people to his sermons at Melodyland. Quoting chapter and verse, he cites Biblical miracles and describes twentieth-century ones. In his book, he writes that he saw eight people who had been restored to life by prayer on a single island in the Pacific. In 1968 he flew from Java to Timor on a cargo plane and then went by jeep to Soa, the island's center of religious activity. Though he was not present when the children and adults were raised from the dead, he vouches for these resurrections, and others in the Philippines and remote areas of Nicaragua and Mexico. He further attests that Timorese evangelists have changed water into wine and walked on water, feats he also did not witness.

At a morning miracle-service a member of his congregation, Denise Beck, told about her escape from death. She and John, her twenty-four-year-old husband, a pilot, took off in his two-passenger plane from Huntington Beach's Meadowlark Airport on December 26, 1976. While flying near Lake Elsinore, en route to Corona, California, the Ercoupe's engine failed, and the plane crashed in a field on the outskirts of Murrietta.

Two hours later a rescue party reached the wreckage. John Beck was dead; Denise, though severely injured, called out, "Help me!" She later recalled that a blackness had enveloped her. She had heard a roar or a buzz and then had seen a brilliant light. Her husband was standing facing Jesus, who towered above him at least ten inches. Jesus's "brownish auburn" hair was long; it touched his shoulders. He wore a pale blue gown and a translucent robe of deeper blue.

John must have changed clothes. He was in the denim suit that he had bought before Christmas, but there were no shoes on his stockinged feet. Denise was happy and would have stayed with them, but Jesus explained the meaning of the Bible to her and sent her back to take care of her young baby and spread God's word.

The Reverend Dr. Wilkerson also tells of a 1977 resurrection in Mexico brought about almost accidentally by the wife of a Melodyland usher. Doris and Phil Smalley were on holiday below the border. An old woman, Margarita Rodriguez, died suddenly in Jarretaderres, a village less than a dozen miles from Puerto Vallarta. Phil Smalley had been asked to take a picture of the body as it rested on a bed in a primitive hut with no floor, walls made from tied wooden sticks, and a roof of corrugated metal.

The covering was taken away from the dead woman's face as Phil adjusted his camera. Later his wife opened the Bible she carried with her and read the twenty-third Psalm, though most of the mourners assembled in the hut could not understand the English words. Carried away by religious fervor, she put one hand on the dead woman's head and began to pray in Spanish—a language she had never studied. The motionless woman began to breathe; then she sat up. When Doris, still speaking words she had never spoken before, asked Señora Rodriguez whether she accepted Jesus, the reply was, "Si, si, si." Senora Rodriguez died "again" the next day and was buried.

The resurrection stories of the Melodyland minister were widely circulated, especially his tales of the marvels in Indonesia. Other evangelists and cult leaders repeated these and similar fabulous accounts of the raising of the dead in faraway places. Some impressionable people believed them and began to think that they too had the power to make the dead live.

Wesley Parker, the youngest of Larry and Alice Parker's four children, was eleven years old in 1973 and had been taking insulin for six years. His parents prayed for him, took him to a healing service at their church, and were sure that the laying on of hands would cure him. When his health seemed to improve, the boy's father stopped the injections, confident that prayers alone could cure the diabetic ailment. Wesley suffered severe abdominal pains, lost consciousness, and died.

Filled with holy zeal, Larry Parker stood by the wooden coffin in Barstow, California, and called on Jesus Christ to resurrect his son. His prayers went unanswered, and the coffin was buried. In four days, Larry Parker said, the boy would rise from the grave. He did not.

Two years later Dorothy Bell's father died at the age of seventy-five. The corpse was kept at her Phoenix Light Temple in Arizona before being taken to various other places and eventually to Payson, when the sect moved there. A hoped-for resurrection did not occur.

Another horror story began on February 2, 1978, when Gladys Rogers, the eighty-year-old mother of interdenominational evangelist Daniel Aaron Rogers, died in Harrison, Arkansas. The woman's body was packed in dry ice for six days and then shipped to a freezer at Clarkson Mortuary in Reeds Spring, Missouri. According to an Associated Press dispatch in the March 13, 1978, New York *Post,* mourners wept, prayed, and sang in the chapel while the dead woman's son and three other preachers conducted resurrection rites over the frozen body in another room.

Evangelist J. T. Williams called for the Lord to raise Gladys Rogers from the dead in so loud a voice that he could be heard in the chapel. "Oh, her eyes are moving," he shouted. "Thank you, Jesus." Later the dead woman's son sadly admitted that he had not seen this happen, but believed that there was still time for her to be revived. Someone in Arkansas had a vision of his mother opening her eyes and arising.

Earlier he had announced that a raiser of the dead from Indonesia would be brought to the chapel if the rites there failed. His mother's resurrection was to be a sign that Christ would return, marking the beginning of a new era. Righteous people would be spared but "the wicked will be burned up . . . by atomic bomb fire."

Seventeen days after the chapel service it was reported that the body had been buried. "I guess the Lord needed mother to be near father more than he wanted her to be with me," evangelist Rogers commented. Because Mrs. Rogers had been frozen in a sitting position, an extra-large casket was needed to hold her icy corpse.

The significance of experiences like those described by Dr. Moody and others was discussed at the 1977 conference of the American Psychological Association in San Francisco. Max Lerner reported in his August 31 column in the New York *Post,* under the heading "Psychologists Ponder Death and Resurrection," that the tantalizing issue had aroused considerable controversy. There was no scientific proof that the dead could be revived or that the living could communicate with them. The response of most of the participants was " 'maybe' or 'not proven,' and at best they suspended their disbelief but did not become believers."

From a vantage point above his own body, Sheldon Ruderman, a delegate, said that he had watched the surgical procedure during a lengthy cancer operation some years earlier.

Ruderman, a counselor at a Berkeley, California, hospital, emphasized that he had been clinically dead at the time.

Robert J. Kastenbaum, from the University of Massachusetts, epitomized the problem: Would psychologists who demanded scientific validation for their other conclusions accept personal stories about encounters with death and psychic manifestations without similar confirmable evidence?

Max Lerner commented that death of two types had been confused—"actual death from which no witness has returned, and a fuzzier kind of death 'encounter.' " The latter was "not the story of Lazarus returned from the dead, but the story of Jacob wrestling with the angel of God, and bearing the marks of his struggle."

Dr. Moody wisely termed the accounts he amassed near-death experiences. Further study by scientists may reveal why and how they occur.

13.

Dr. Elisabeth Kübler-Ross

A prayer was offered for Dr. Elisabeth Kübler-Ross during the 1977 conference of the Spiritual Frontiers Fellowship in Kansas City, Missouri. The assembled clergymen and lay people admired the expert on death and dying. They shared her conviction that the soul survives, but it is doubtful that any believed, as she now seemed to, that a dead woman could miraculously reappear in the flesh and walk, talk, and write like an ordinary human.

The psychiatrist's inspiring books *On Death and Dying* (1969), *Questions and Answers on Death and Dying* (1974), and *Death—the Final Stage of Growth* (1975) brought a new understanding of an old problem to those who read them. Millions more learned about the pioneering achievements of this small woman with just a trace of a foreign accent from her television and radio interviews. Articles in newspapers and popular magazines, as well as her lectures and seminars, spread her fame across the nation.

The first of triplets and the frailest, weighing about two pounds, she was born in Zürich in 1926. In a chapter contributed to Jess E. Weiss's *The Vestibule,* she recalled an eerie story that her mother had told her. When very young, her mother had entered the church alone after the older people had left to prepare for the burial of her great-grandmother. The child approached the open coffin for a last look at the aged lady. Under the corpse's chin was a "churchbook," as was the custom in the village. The girl was about to kiss her for the last time when the old woman raised her chin, and the book slid away.

This sign of life saved the old woman from a premature burial. Between that day and the one eight years later when she really died, she would talk to only one person, the little girl whose alert eyes had given her those extra years. Death, she said on many occasions, "was a peaceful existence"; it was the fear of entering it that disturbed people.

As a child, Elisabeth herself visited a neighbor dying from injuries sustained when he fell from a tree. He always greeted her with a smile. His only worry was that he would not be there to harvest the crop on his farm.

World War II and Nazi atrocities cast a dark shadow on neutral Switzerland. Zürich had a large Germanic population. Refugees fled there from the north and east with tales of horrors. A volunteer on days when she was not at school, Elisabeth helped treat the sick, lame, and wounded. The day that peace came she was on the roof of the hospital with them, listening to the sound of church bells pealing out from the towers of the city.

She realized the extent of the destruction when she again volunteered, this time to go to Poland to nurse survivors of the Holocaust. Memories of what she saw in a former concentration camp haunted her dreams even after she received her medical degree from the University of Zürich and married another physician, Dr. Emanuel Robert Ross.

Dr. Kübler-Ross told Herbert Mitgang, when he interviewed her for the November 27, 1977, "Behind the Best Sellers" column of the *New York Times Book Review,* that she had planned to become a general practitioner, a country doctor, in Switzerland. Instead, she worked as an intern in a Glen Cove, New York, hospital, as a resident at Manhattan State Hospital, and as a psychiatry instructor in University of Colorado and University of Chicago hospitals.

She developed her method for easing the anxiety of terminally ill patients, their families, and close friends by talking
with them about their problems and by heeding advice from
clergymen, social workers, and other people with experience
in the field. She learned that most patients knew when they
were about to die and that those who were fortunate enough
to recover after nearing the brink of death no longer dreaded
it. She became convinced that death was only another phase
of life, for which patients and those who loved them could
prepare if they tried to understand it.

Her books, death-and-dying workshops, and lectures have
had an enormous impact. Death is now discussed as frankly
as sex on television and radio talk-shows. There are even
courses on this once taboo topic in some schools. The March
14, 1977, issue of *Newsweek* reported on a nine-week "Atti-
tudes Toward Death" series at the Miami Beach Senior High
School in Florida. The one hundred eighty students who
elected to take it read relevant passages from Shakespeare,
Edgar Allan Poe, and William Faulkner. They wrote obituary
notices about themselves, visited mortuaries, observed embalming procedures, and exchanged opinions about the con-
sequences of biological military weapons and hara kiri. When
three students lost their lives in a tragic accident, their friends
movingly expressed their feelings to their classmates. Until
then, they had not realized how much their emotions would
be affected.

Unexpected news of the death of a loved one can have
an even stronger impact on a survivor when this information
is conveyed by a psychic. Dr. Kübler-Ross's mother had been
in a Swiss hospital for four years, paralyzed by a stroke. An
American medium jolted the psychiatrist by stating that the
woman was dead. Dr. Kübler-Ross doubted this. Someone
would have cabled or telephoned her immediately. Yet, she
listened, heart pounding, as her "mother" spoke through
the medium.

She thought of her visits to her mother's bedside. Though
her mother could not speak, she could give yes or no replies

to questions by moving her eyelids. The psychiatrist wondered whether she could have helped in some way to alleviate the suffering. Her "mother" seemed to know what she was thinking. She said that her daughter had not asked about the headache that was causing her pain. A medication might have relieved it.

Later that day word came from Europe that her mother had died. The thought that she had unwittingly contributed to her mother's agony preyed on the sensitive psychiatrist's mind. She asked another doctor with more knowledge of stroke paralysis whether a patient in this condition could have a headache. He answered emphatically that this was not possible. She responded heatedly, "Listen, if my mother said she had a headache, she had a headache!" Dr. Kübler-Ross told James Crenshaw about this outburst when he interviewed her for the April 1977 issue of *Fate* magazine. She also told him about her strange encounter with a living dead woman.

She had earlier described the woman in her contribution to Weiss's *The Vestibule*. Mrs. S. had been afflicted with Parkinson's disease, a progressively debilitating and usually fatal intestinal ailment, for twenty of her more than fifty years. Her psychotic husband constantly abused their son, and she was determined to arrange for a relative to look after the boy before she died. Mrs. S. had been in the intensive care units of several medical institutions and, at one of Dr. Kübler-Ross's workshops, was eager to tell of her most remarkable experience.

Weakened by internal bleeding, Mrs. S. said, she had lost consciousness. She heard later that a nurse opened the door, saw her seemingly lifeless body, and ran for aid. When awareness returned to Mrs. S., she was floating above her own body. She watched the efforts being made to resuscitate her and saw every person in the room. They seemed distressed, and she wished that she could calm them.

Blacking out again, she reentered her body as it was being wheeled to the morgue. She tugged away the sheet that was covering her head. The startled attendants quickly changed the direction of the conveyance. No one, however, asked her what had happened. It was obvious that she felt better after talking about this fantastic occurrence and discussing it with her listeners. She was even happier when, in reply to a direct question, Dr. Kübler-Ross said that she did not consider her to be psychotic. Mrs. S. was able to complete the arrangements for her son's future before she died.

That was how the story appeared in the book, but there was more to it, as James Crenshaw discovered during his interview. Dr. Kübler-Ross told him that her constant work with the dying had subjected her to a tremendous strain. In 1968 she decided to concentrate on another branch of medicine. Standing in a hospital corridor near a clergyman friend as he waited for the elevator, she turned to tell him about this decision.

Before she could speak, Mrs. S. materialized beside her. The dead woman was as real as the minister. The clergyman entered the elevator; Mrs. S. went with Dr. Kübler-Ross to her office. Sitting in the chair on the far side of the desk, Mrs. S. made her promise to go on with her compassionate mission. Perhaps not trusting her senses, Dr. Kübler-Ross asked the visitor from the afterlife to write a note to another physician whom she had met at the workshop. Mrs. S.'s smile suggested that she knew the reason for the request—concrete evidence that Mrs. S. had been there. She wrote a message, then the living dead woman left, not by dissolving in a misty haze, but by walking out through the open door.

While Mrs. S. appeared in the flesh, Dr. Kübler-Ross has also communed with more traditional spirits, as Eleanor Links Hoover noted in the March 1977 issue of *Human Behavior.* Speaking at a holistic healing meeting in San Diego, California, the psychiatrist casually mentioned that the previous night she had consulted with three invisible entities about the subject matter of her address. "Tell them about us," had been the immediate reply.

An insight into the development of Dr. Kübler-Ross's involvement with psychic phenomena came in November 1977, when an interview that Peggy Taylor and Rick Ingrasci had

had with her during the Rocky Mountain Healing Arts Festival in August was printed in the magazine *New Age.* Three years earlier, she had told them, the pressures of one of her five-day seminars had exhausted her. There were more than sixty in attendance—patients, parents whose children were dying, several people recently bereaved, medical and social workers, and students of philosophy and yoga. The sessions extended from early morning to far past midnight.

At first the people participating were evasive as to why they were there. When the barrier of self-reserve was broken, their guilts, hopes, and fears were released. There were tears and angry accusations, directed at Dr. Kübler-Ross and others. Eventually harmony came as the participants reached a fuller understanding of both life and death.

Late the last night there was a ceremony and a celebration. Everyone gathered around a blazing bonfire and tossed cones from a pine tree into the flames, symbolizing the rejection of negative aspects of their personalities. As they sat by the fire eating freshly baked bread and drinking wine, ego wounds were healed and an exuberant emotion of oneness with God and nature prevailed.

At 5 A.M. the tired psychiatrist tried to leave, but a dying patient insisted that she hold her hand. After doing so for perhaps fifteen minutes, she went to her room. With luck she could sleep soundly and be up at seven. As soon as she was in bed, the door was flung open by a young woman who had been deeply moved by the fireside rites. The rising of the sun would mark her birthday, she said—not the anniversary of the day she had been born, but the beginning of a new life. She asked the psychiatrist who had made this epic event possible to join her as the rays of the sun drove the darkness from the sky. Too fatigued to get up, Dr. Kübler-Ross told the woman that she could sit by her window.

Almost as soon as the psychiatrist closed her eyes, her inner self was propelled from her body. Floating above it, she relaxed and saw a fabulous sight. Spirits, working as efficiently as mechanics on an automobile assembly line, removed tired and worn parts from her and replaced them with new material. Ninety minutes later she awakened in bed, feeling younger and better than she had in years. The mouth of the birthday celebrant by the window was agape. She told Dr. Kübler-Ross that she had stopped breathing. Anyone who did not know about out-of-the-body experiences would have been sure that she was dead.

After this incredible episode Dr. Kübler-Ross began reading books about others who had left their bodies. There are many on this controversial subject. Hereward Carrington based a chapter of his *Modern Psychical Phenomena* (1919) on a massive French manual—Dr. Charles Lancelin's *Méthode de dédoublement personnel: extérioration de la neuricité: sorties en astral.* Then, in collaboration with Sylvan Muldoon, an American who claimed to have made the first of dozens of flights at the age of twelve, Carrington wrote *The Projection of the Astral Body* (1929), followed by *The Phenomena of Astral Projection* (1931).

Dr. Robert Crookall, a British geologist, issued *The Study and Practice of Astral Projection* in 1961, and he has discussed more than a thousand cases in various later books. Celia Green, director of the Institute of Psychophysical Research in Oxford, England, analyzed the responses of some four hundred people who answered a call for information on those who had had *Out-of-the-Body Experiences* in a book with this title in 1968. There is considerable anecdotal evidence, but no scientific proof that the consciousness-separation process actually occurs.

Dr. Charles T. Tart tells in the 1977 book *PSI Scientific Studies of the Psychic Realm* of an informal experiment with a man in Virginia, Robert Monroe, who attempted to travel in the spirit to the University of California psychologist's home in Davis. Judging from what Monroe claimed to have seen, Dr. Tart concluded that Monroe made the cross-country spirit trip, but then looked in on the wrong house.

Monroe is a man of imagination and action. He has written and produced radio shows, was once a vice-president of the Mutual Broadcasting System, and now owns his own station in Winston-Salem, North Carolina, and a 640-acre estate in Charlottesville, Virginia. He had his initial consciousness-separation experience in 1958. He has told of this and subsequent astral adventures in *Journeys Out of the Body* (1971). Classes for those who yearn to travel without bodily encumbrances are conducted in a building on his property.

Dr. Kübler-Ross said in the November 1977 issue of *New Age* that she went to Charlottesville two years after the spirit workmen had repaired her body. Her first out-of-the-body experience had not been premeditated. She was eager to learn whether she could schedule them at will. She and the other students reclined on a waterbed in an isolated room. Wires ran from the electrodes on her head to a polygraph. Sounds amplified to induce the proper mood reached her through earphones.

She was comfortable on the waterbed as she awaited the take-off signal. When it came, she speedily and effortlessly ascended. She knew that it was possible to penetrate the ceiling when she reached it, but, as she had never tried to do this before, she studied the texture. The instructor's voice brought her abruptly back into her body. Though she tried to break free again during this session, she did not succeed.

Students were encouraged to speak up in the discussions following each lesson. She complained that the instructor had interrupted a marvelous flight. Hereafter, when the instruments showed that she had reached the right consciousness level, he should let her soar.

Firmly believing that she could master the technique of quick detachment, she intended to zoom up into the clouds on the following day. Resting again on the waterbed, primed by her urge to project, she took off like a rocket and shot through the ceiling and into the sky. Streaking far above the earth, she suddenly remembered that she had not followed one of the basic instructions. She was traveling horizontally, not vertically. No problem. She tilted herself up into the right position without losing speed.

In the far reaches of outer space, beyond the areas explored by astronauts, she became exhilarated. Traveling in a vast, uncharted celestial realm, she saw sights no one else had ever seen and heard somewhere in the distance two words, "Shanti Nilaya," being repeated again and again.

She returned to her body refreshed, elated, and vibrant. She had accomplished what she had set out to do. Someone in Virginia told her that Shanti meant peace, but Nilaya was still a mystery—until she went to Berkeley, California. There she was informed that the words were a Sanscrit term for "ultimate home of peace." Late in 1977 Dr. Kübler-Ross established an institute for the terminally ill in Valley Center, California. She called it Shanti Nilaya.

Dr. Kübler-Ross told the *New Age* interviewers that she had sensed the presence of an unseen force in the secluded house in which she had stayed while taking the out-of-the-body course on Robert Monroe's estate in Virginia. As a child in Switzerland she had no dread of such things; she didn't believe in them. She knew better now. The books on the occult that she had read and her experiences with mediums and mystics had increased her awareness.

She was sure that she was being watched as she took a shower, so she bolted the door of her bedroom before going to bed. When she awoke, the door was open. It was well past 1 A.M. when she returned for her second night in the house on a hillside in the woods. She realized that it was useless to lock the doors; still, she turned on a light on the porch and one near the bed before she pulled back the covers and eased under them.

Keyed up by her projection into outer space that day, she rolled and tossed as she tried to sleep. Then she became delirious, suffering the final throes of every patient she had ever treated—the searing pains, the intestinal aches, the undescribable agonies—not once, but again and again. Though she could scarcely breathe, she called for sympathy, a man's shoulder on which to rest her head. A voice spoke, denying her this consolation. She pleaded for the touch of a comforting hand. None came, not even a finger.

Finally she understood that she had to seek for greater knowledge alone. When she was ready, the lining of her abdomen began to shake, vibrating faster and faster. Then her body vibrated, a closet vibrated, the walls vibrated, finally the earth and the universe. Images began to form: a vagina, a lotus bud. The bud began to blossom. A light as brilliant as the sun rose behind it. The flower opened fully. Its beauty dazzled her. Then the room stopped vibrating, the vision faded, and she slept.

In the morning when Dr. Kübler-Ross left the house on the hillside, she felt as though she was not walking on the pebbled path, but gliding lightly above it.

What is one to make of fantastic tales like these? Obviously Dr. Kübler-Ross believes that she had these experiences. Is there a rational explanation for them? A medium told her that her mother had died, and she was chided for ignoring her mother's headaches; she became fascinated with accounts of psychic phenomena. Some people read books on diseases and imagine that they have every symptom described. Others read stories of the occult and are sure that they too have mysterious powers.

The mind is susceptible to suggestive influences. Perceptions are altered by beliefs. Psychiatrists and psychoanalysts interpret dreams and fantasies as reflections or aspirations, fears or repressed emotions.

Dr. Elisabeth Kübler-Ross merits high praise for her compassionate work with the dying. Her empathy lightens their emotional burdens and enables the terminally ill and those who love them to deal more effectively with issues all too often ignored.

Many of her friends are distressed by her fascination with more esoteric areas. One who expressed concern was told that this was a sign of his own insecurity and that those who dare to venture beyond the known are always misunderstood. One need not be a psychiatrist to understand that the course of her life has changed and that the prayer said for her by those attending the 1977 conference of the Spiritual Frontiers Fellowship was for a humanitarian who in recent years seems to have strayed beyond the remotest boundary of their faith.

14.

Death and
Near-Death

In clinical death the heart stops pulsating and the lungs cease functioning. Biological death comes with irrevocable chemical changes and cellular destruction. Efficient treatment or accidental occurrences can reactivate clinically dead bodies. Heart transplants are made with organs that are clinically but not biologically dead. Advocates of cryonics—preservation by freezing—hope that cures for fatal diseases will be discovered in the future and that the frozen dead will be thawed, treated, and returned to life.

As the first body to be prepared for cryonic suspension was not encapsulated until 1967 and as no attempt has been made to revitalize it or others now in cold storage, the results of what at the moment is an unproven theory can only be conjectured. Meanwhile, an onslaught against the ravages of biological death is being made by specially trained paramedics in many cities. Rescue teams, equipped with scientific devices carried in speedy ambulances, are on the alert for life-saving missions twenty-four hours a day.

Responding to an emergency call in 1977, paramedics from Beekman-Downtown Hospital rushed with their gear from a tenth floor elevator of Manhattan's Municipal Building. A physician in the crowded hallway told them that there was no need to hurry. The man who had collapsed in the corridor was dead. Undeterred, the paramedics set up their equipment and began cardiopulmonary stimulation. Oxygen fed through a throat tube, drugs dripped intravenously, and spaced electric jolts kept the body functioning biologically for forty-five minutes. Then the portable electrocardiogram indicated that a normal heart beat had been restored. People who had been watching the resuscitative procedure spontaneously applauded.

Paramedic Ed Stapleton told a *New York Times* reporter, who wrote the story of the dramatic incident on May 30, that in the year and a half he had been teamed with Tony Ciociari, they had responded to approximately one hundred crisis calls. Only three patients had been taken to the hospital; the others were revived on the scene—except when those phoning for assistance had delayed too long before dialing.

Prompt on-the-scene action by another paramedic restored a fifty-four-year-old messenger to life after firemen pulled his body through a window of a smoke-filled room in a Bayport, Long Island, boarding house in 1979. In fifteen minutes Daniel Gallagher was breathing again. Ralph Scofield, a paramedic with the Community Ambulance Service, said that this was the first of four resuscitations of Gallagher. He told a New York *Post* reporter on January 10 that the patient's pulse stopped for a second and third time while they were en route to Brookhaven Memorial Hospital. Scofield gave mouth to mouth resuscitation as he changed oxygen tanks. A fourth cardiac arrest occurred in the hospital's emergency room. Again prompt treatment saved Gallagher's life.

An observant GI embalmer prevented the premature burial of a severely wounded American soldier in Vietnam in 1967. Sp 4c Jacky C. Bayne, serving with the 196th Light Infantry Brigade near Chu Lai, had been walking across a field with an army dog when a land mine exploded. Medics removing shrapnel from Bayne's motionless body could detect no sign of cardiac or pulmonary activity. Hours later, when the embalmer made an incision, weak but regular wrist pulsations signaled that the "corpse" was alive. Bayne recovered in a hospital, where blood transfusions and other restorative measures were applied. Eventually the twenty-two-year-old patient was flown back to South Carolina. A portion of his brain had been damaged, but despite the long span between clinical death and resuscitation he had survived.

There were so many reports of premature burials in the nineteenth century that Joseph O. Barrett crusaded for delayed interments in his book *Looking Beyond: A Souvenir of Love to the Bereft* (1871). The common custom of burial within three days of presumed death was, he charged, "reckless and unpardonable." Barrett, a spiritualist, claimed that it often took five days or more for a soul to detach itself from a body.

Numerous accounts of unexpected revivals were printed in American newspapers. E. M. Boshiller traveled from Elkhart, Indiana, to Lagrange in August 1889 to have a grave dug for his dead daughter. On his return the child was alive; she had begun breathing again during his absence.

A man in Boston had been put into a coffin. The undertaker, hammering at a nail protruding from the interior drapery, struck the nailhead so forcibly that it flew off and hit the chin of the corpse. The supposedly dead man sat up and complained. In August 1901 a hearse carrying a casket containing the body of Julia McPresz, a five-year-old Hanston, Kansas, child, to a graveyard in Larned, was struck by lightning. The bolt killed two horses, knocked the driver of the hearse from his seat, ripped through the side of the vehicle, and tore away the top of the casket. Members of the funeral procession said that they saw the little girl sit up and begin crying.

The only certain proof of death is bodily decomposition, according to John R. Meader and Hereward Carrington, the authors of *Death: Its Causes and Phenomena* (1911). They noted that the Marquis d'Ourches had posted two awards with the French Academy of Medicine for some simple, sure signal of the cessation of life; one award was of twenty thousand francs, the other of five thousand francs. Entries had been received from 102 physicians. None merited the larger sum;

the smaller was shared by six contestants. The first of these wrote about how the flame of a candle affected the finger of a dying patient. The second described the gray spots he had seen in the eyes of the dying; the third, a different sort of pupil discoloration. The fourth discoursed on the lividity of cadavers. The fifth and sixth reported on the temperatures of those approaching death.

Physicians today say that clinical death occurs when neither heartbeat nor respiration can be measured and when restorative techniques have no effect. Brain death follows. When, during a twenty-four hour period, no trace of brain activity can be measured with an electroencephalograph (EEG), death is irrevocable. There is no precise moment of death; various parts of the body die at different times.

Until 1970 no American state had a law defining death. Then Kansas enacted a statute that offered two criteria— one, the permanent cessation of heart and respiratory system functions; the other, the permanent cessation of brain activity. These determinations were to be made by physicians. Two years later Maryland adopted a similar statute.

Though a person may be medically and legally dead, some people think that eventually—if the body has been properly prepared and stored—the person may live again in the same physical housing. Dr. Alexis Carrel, a noted member of the Rockefeller Institute for Medical Research, predicted in 1935 that at least a few humans, placed in a state of suspended animation, might enjoy life in several centuries.

Dr. Carrel's lecture that year on "The Mysteries of Death" attracted the largest crowd on record to the New York Academy of Medicine. A front-page story in the *New York Times* on December 13 reported his theories. The short, chubby surgeon-biologist explained that death did not come quickly. When a man was stabbed in the heart, blood flowed from the wound. Eventually circulation stopped and respiration ceased. Though legally dead, he was not "hopelessly dead." He could be resuscitated because his brain and other organs were still functioning. Without treatment, this pseudo death would be followed by actual death, caused by the disintegration of the vital parts. Each died at a different time, first the brain, then the other essential cellular structures. The mind usually went first. Less important organs could exist for several hours.

Spiritualists claimed that the soul survives the death of the body, Dr. Carrel said, but he believed that the soul and the body were one. He also believed that clairvoyants could perceive the past and the future. "Therefore it is not possible to make a distinction between the survival of a psychic principle and a phenomenon of clairvoyance." He was aware that "hundreds of millions of people believe in the immortality of the soul. Such a faith belongs in the domain of religion and philosophy, not in that of experimental science."

Despite this disavowal of theological and philosophical doctrines, Dr. Carrel said that lifespans might be extended almost indefinitely. Some small animals, for example the arthropod, "stop their metabolism when they are dried." Weeks later, on being moistened, they revive and function normally. Alexander Lipschutz, another researcher, had grafted partially dried organs into live guinea pigs. These implants had kept their structure and continued their glandular activities. Less hazardous ways of maintaining life in tissues would be found.

Looking far into the future, Dr. Carrel said, "Some individuals could be put into storage for long periods of time, brought back to normal existence for other periods, and permitted in this manner to live for several centuries. We should remember the utopias of today are the realities of tomorrow."

The eminent researcher who made this prophecy had been born in France, near Lyons, in 1873. As a university undergraduate, he read books and periodicals dealing with psychic phenomena, as well as the texts required for his degree. One of his early heroes was Dr. Charles Richet, a noted physiologist who actively pursued another career as an investigator of spirit mediums and the occult.

The surgeon-to-be acquired great digital dexterity as a student. He could tie knots in catgut so firmly with one hand that two could not loosen them. His skill with a needle was prodigious. He could take five hundred tiny stitches in a single piece of flimsy cigarette paper. His doctoral thesis described how he had sliced away the tumor of an ailing cat, flipped over the thyroid gland, and then replaced it in such a way that, in this reversed position, it functioned perfectly.

After a brief period as a surgeon in French hospitals, he spent a year in a laboratory at McGill Hospital in Montreal, another at the University of Chicago, and then, in 1906, went to work for the Rockefeller Institute for Medical Research. He was the first surgeon in the United States to be awarded the Nobel Prize. His 1912 description of his techniques was so terse that it took less than two typed pages. He had perfected a new method of sewing the open ends of severed arteries and veins. Three punctures made with a needle threaded with Vaselined silk were sufficient to close the tubes when the thread was drawn tight and secured.

The following year Dr. Carrel read that his early idol, Dr. Charles Richet had also become a Nobel Prize laureate. Dr. Carrel returned to France, serving as a lieutenant in World War I. Promoted to major, he ran a hospital at Compiègne. There he developed a system of pumping antiseptic into severe wounds that was to save the lives of thousands of Allied soldiers.

Yet, until his *Man, the Unknown* was published in 1935, the public knew little about him except that he had worked with Colonel Charles A. Lindbergh to construct a heart pump and that since 1913 he had kept the heart of a chicken alive in a glass bottle.

Dr. Raymond Pearl, a Johns Hopkins University biologist, assessed the controversial book in the September 29, 1935, issue of the *New York Times Book Review*. "For probably the first time in history," Professor Pearl wrote, "the Soul has taken a duly appointed place in a first-rate professional treatise on biology." Dr. Carrel referred to this "profoundly mysterious entity as "the aspect of ourselves that is specific of our nature and distinguishes man from all other animals."

No one should question such mystical experiences as "a journey of the soul beyond the dimensions of our world and its union with a higher reality."

Professor Pearl pointed out that this was just a sample of Dr. Carrel's ramblings in an otherwise commendable volume. To the reviewer's amazement, clairvoyance, telepathy, and miraculous cures were "discussed seriously as integral and important parts of human biology." Dr. Carrel's colleagues would be "shocked and pained" when they read these pronouncements.

The public, however, became intrigued. Two thousand people were turned away from the doors of the Academy of Medicine when the distinguished surgeon talked about death, psychics, and suspended animation. Dr. Anson Julius Carlson, a noted physiologist in whose laboratory at the University of Chicago the surgeon had once been employed, denounced Dr. Carrel's statements. There were no proven facts regarding telepathy, clairvoyance, and alleged spirit phenomena, Dr. Carlson said. As to bodies being preserved for hundreds of years in a state of suspended animation, neither science nor medicine would endorse this theory.

"It is well known," Dr. Carlson told Associated Press reporter John Lear, "that life in individual organs and tissues may by suitable means be maintained for some time after the man as an individual has died. But biology and medicine know of no resurrection of the individual man, after disease or accident has destroyed one necessary link in the life process of that individual."

After this interview appeared in print, a story from Russia reported that a man had been brought back to life three hours after his death. Earlier, the Central Institute of Blood Transfer in Moscow had resuscitated dead animals. Now with a pumping device invented by Dr. Sergai Brukhanenko, a professor at the institute, a man who had strangled himself with a noose and who had been clinically dead for three hours, breathed, opened his eyes, and showed other signs of animation—for two minutes.

Perhaps inspired by the brief success in Moscow, Dr. Robert Cornish, a Berkeley, California, scientist petitioned the governors of three states for permission to revive convicts who had been sentenced to die in gas chambers. He said that he had resuscitated six dogs—including one that had been clinically dead for thirteen days—with drug injections and manual pressure. The animals, Dr. Cornish admitted, had not fully recovered, though one had swallowed food placed in its mouth, blinked its eyes, and wagged its tail. The governors ignored Dr. Cornish's petitions.

Proposed resurrections could create several problems, as Dr. Louis E. Bisch, professor of neuropsychiatry at Polyclinic Medical School and Hospital in New York, pointed out: "What man can be sure of his inheritance if his dead father or his dead uncle may return from his sepulcher days, weeks, or years after his burial? . . . What ruler can be sure of his throne if his predecessor may enter the coronation hall and snatch the crown from his head?" Would it be fair to the poor, Dr. Bisch asked, if only the rich could afford to pay for the luxury of revitalization? Certainly the cost of resurrection would be greater than that of birth or burial.

This assumption remains valid. Fees for cryonic suspensions, including the freezing and encapsulating of clinically dead bodies, were $15,000, and annual storage and upkeep charges were $1,800, according to an article by Kathleen Stein in the October 1978 issue of *Omni,* a monthly magazine of science fiction and fact.

Dr. Robert C. W. Ettinger, a physics instructor, published the basic book on cryonics in 1962. Since then, his *Prospect of Immortality,* revised in 1964, has led to the establishment of several body-freezing centers.

The first human to make arrangements for long-term encapsulation, Dr. James H. Bedford, a Los Angeles psychologist, died in 1967. The foundation that he had established for the purpose saw to it that his chilled body was drained of blood, his lungs and arteries treated with chemical solutions, and his body wrapped in sheets of aluminum foil. Eventually the body was encased in a vacuum capsule, which had been constructed in Phoenix, Arizona. Liquid nitrogen pumped into the container maintained a temperature of minus 196 degrees centigrade. Since then, another capsule has replaced the original one, which developed a leak, and the capsule has been shuttled from southern California to the San Francisco Bay area and back.

No one seems to know how many bodies have been placed in cryonic suspension since the initial venture. It is estimated that more than twenty and less than thirty have been encapsulated. Several are said to have been removed and buried underground in more conventional containers.

Dr. David Robinson, a Georgetown University cryobiologist, has frozen and thawed heart cells of rats and chickens and is experimenting with organs, in the hope that they can be preserved for transplant operations. He admitted in the Washington *Post* magazine of October 8, 1978, that as yet "we can't even freeze a piece of skin let alone a whole heart or human without producing some damage." He described the corpses in cryonic suspension as "nothing more than frozen meat and bone."

Even the most earnest cryonics advocates have not volunteered to be frozen alive. Dr. Alexis Carrel's 1935 prediction of humans being revived periodically from suspended animation to sample life in several centuries is as remote a possibility today as it was when he made it.

15.

Souls
and Mrs. Piper

William James, the Harvard psychologist, wrote the first scientific report on Leonora Piper, the American medium who later convinced Sir Oliver Lodge, Dr. Richard Hodgson, Professor George Hervey Hyslop, and other distinguished investigators that souls survived death, retained memories, conversed through her vocal chords, and wrote using her hand. Professor James had no doubt about Mrs. Piper's supernormal powers, but he admitted that he could not explain them.

Mrs. Piper has been acclaimed as the greatest trance medium who ever lived. If she really conveyed messages from the dead, she merits the praise she has received. If, on the other hand, she acquired her information from other sources, a study of her career is still worthwhile as a demonstration of how her sitters' will to believe blunted their critical judgments.

Thousands of pages in the publications of the English Society for Psychical Research and the American Society for Psychical Research are filled with lengthy accounts of this medium's séances and the attempts made to analyze her talents. During the years that members of these organizations supervised her sittings, many clients came to her under assumed names; at least one hid his face with a mask until a spirit communicator identified him.

During the first phase of Mrs. Piper's mediumship (1884–92), the tall, well-proportioned young woman with brown hair and blue eyes relaxed in a comfortable chair, grasping a seated patron's hands. Breathing deeply, she trembled and convulsively contorted. Gradually her facial expressions and gestures became more masculine. When she spoke, it was with a deeper, harsher voice that had a trace of a French accent.

Her principal spirit control, Dr. Phinuit, claimed that he had been a physician in Metz many years before. He named names, sometimes of almost forgotten relatives; he told of obscure incidents that sitters acknowledged were true. After identifying an ill child or relative, he recommended remedies. Frequently he expressed unspoken thoughts before the sitters could put them into words.

Such was the case with William James's mother-in-law, who returned from her first visit to Mrs. Piper in the fall of 1885 completely perplexed. The entranced medium had called out the Christian names of many members of her family and shown an amazing familiarity with their activities. The psychologist's sister-in-law went to see the medium the following day; she was even more bewildered. Mrs. Piper had held a letter written in Italian pressed to her brow and accurately described the man who had sent it.

Professor James, a member of the Committee on Mediumistic Phenomena of the American Society for Psychical Research, had listened to many similar stories; often they were exaggerated. As no member of the committee had mentioned Mrs. Piper, he and his wife were eager to assess her marvels for themselves. The medium lived in Arlington Heights, once called West Cambridge, a few miles from their house.

Most of the family information that had impressed the psychologist's mother-in-law and sister-in-law was mentioned again as the Jameses listened to Dr. Phinuit. He also spelled out a surname he had not given before, that of Professor

James's father-in-law, Gibbens. Phinuit first gave it as Niblin or Giblin, then finally, after much effort, got it right. He had trouble too with Herman, the first name of the professor's son, who had died a year earlier, spelling it Herrin.

Professor James participated in eleven more séances and then studied the accounts of twenty-four sitters whom he had sent to Arlington Heights and one by a person who had gone without his instigation. Reporting on his findings for the 1886 *Proceedings of the American Society for Psychical Research,* he rejected the possibility that the medium or an associate had gathered data on her clients; he accepted her trances as unfeigned. His conclusion: "I now believe her to be in possession of a power as yet unexplained."

The psychic who perplexed the psychologist had been born near Nashua, New Hampshire. She was the wife of William Piper, a clerk in a large Boston store. Unfortunately, he is mentioned only in passing in the chronicles of Leonora's mediumship; it would be interesting to know more about his interests and his reaction to his wife's phenomena.

In 1884, shortly after the birth of their first daughter, Mrs. Piper attended the public meetings of J. R. Cocke, a sightless medium, who was said to have great healing powers and who conducted development classes for prospective clairvoyants.

Cocke touched Leonora, who lost consciousness, scrawled a message on a piece of paper, and gave it to the most prominent person in the room, a Judge Frost. The judge, a spiritualist of thirty years standing, proclaimed the words to be from his dead son and said that the message was the most significant he had ever received from the other side. Soon afterwards, Mrs. Piper became a professional medium, charging fees for putting survivors in touch with their dead loved ones. Her quick success as a psychic enabled her and her husband to move to the suburbs.

Her first spirit guide was an Indian girl who said that her name was Chlorine. Then Henry Wadsworth Longfellow, the poet; Johann Sebastian Bach, the composer; Mrs. Sarah Siddons, the actress; and Commodore Cornelius Vanderbilt, the

financier, spoke through her vocal chords before her dominant control became Dr. Phinuit. (Sitters at J. R. Cocke's
meetings recalled that the blind healer's spirit guide had been
a French physician who pronounced his name Finné or Fin-
net.) Mrs. Piper's Phinuit had a very limited knowledge of
his native tongue, as did the medium. He communicated in
English, but not in the speech patterns of a Frenchman using
a second language.

Even Mrs. Piper's most ardent patrons admitted that the
guide had a "stagey" accent. Yet he seemed to know more
about their problems and some of their relatives than they
did themselves. He was an excellent listener, and the remedies he prescribed for their ailments often worked. Medical
men who went to séances with their wives were shocked to
find that Dr. Phinuit did not recognize the Latin terms for
the potions he recommended.

Two weeks after Dr. Richard Hodgson arrived in Boston
in May 1887 to take the post of secretary and chief investigator of the psychical research society, Professor James escorted
him to a Piper séance. Enthralled by the revelations that
he heard through Dr. Phinuit, Dr. Hodgson would spend
the rest of his life documenting the case which just might
prove that souls survive after death.

Born in Australia, Hodgson, after graduating from the University of Melbourne, had sailed to England, where he studied
and lectured on law at Cambridge University. An early member of the Society for Psychical Research, he displayed great
skill in exposing the frauds practiced by Madame Blavatsky,
the theosophist. Sent by the society to India to study the
alleged miracles performed by the Russian mystic, he wrote
a devastating account of her deceptions that established him
as the most perceptive psychical researcher of his day.

The arrival of the bearded thirty-two-year-old Australian
in Boston had been hailed by Mrs. Piper's advocates as well
as her disparagers. Those who believed that she had a supernormal power hoped that Hodgson would define it; those
who held a differing opinion were sure that he would reveal

how she cheated. Meanwhile, Professor James had been too busy with academic and literary matters to make a really thorough investigation himself.

Mrs. Piper did not cause tables to float, as had Eusapia Palladino, an Italian medium exposed by Dr. Hodgson, nor did she materialize letters from mahatmas in the manner of Madame Blavatsky. Ghostly forms never appeared in her presence, as they did when Helen Berry, another New England medium, became entranced. The single question for the investigators was whether Mrs. Piper's information came from the spirit world or from a more material source.

Dr. Hodgson published lengthy reports on Mrs. Piper's phenomena in volumes eight and thirteen of the *Proceedings of the Society for Psychical Research.* From the start her trance knowledge of his personal life had astonished him. He arranged for fifty people whom she had never met to attend sittings. "Most of these persons," he wrote, "were told facts through the trance-utterances which they felt sure could not have become known to Mrs. Piper by ordinary means." At the insistence of a skeptical member of the Boston society, private detectives were hired for three weeks to see whether they could find any way by which the medium or her husband might gather data secretly. The shadowers were as baffled as the sitters.

Several members of the British society, eager to study Mrs. Piper's mediumship themselves, brought her to England with her two young daughters. (She refused to leave Boston without them.) Arrangements were made for her to give eighty-three séances under close supervision. An extensive account of her first visit to Britain appeared in the sixth volume of the society's *Proceedings.*

Oliver Lodge, then professor of physics at University College in Liverpool, met the travelers soon after the Cunard steamship *Scythia* docked on November 19, 1889. He did not introduce himself by name, but later remembered mentioning that he too had children—seven of them. He sat with the medium for the first time in F. W. H. Myers's home in Cambridge. While Mrs. Piper held Lodge's hands in one room, Myers, the secretary of the society, took notes behind a curtain in an adjoining chamber.

When the medium began talking in the voice of Dr. Phinuit, Lodge asked, "Can you tell me about my relations?" Phinuit replied, "I get your mother's influence. She's very near to you, a good mother to you."

"Yes, she was," the physicist confirmed. This comment, Lodge noted in the *Proceedings,* "stupidly" revealed that his mother was dead. The medium's spirit control went on to say that Lodge's father had also entered the afterlife, along with an uncle, his mother's brother.

Lodge asked for the name of this uncle. Phinuit did not give it; instead he began asking questions himself: "Who's Alfred?" "Do you know Margaret?" This is a technique known as fishing. (If the sitter bites—identifies a name, or adds a comment—the medium usually utilizes this data, then or later.) Lodge denied knowing a Margaret, an Uncle William, or a Thomas, "grandfather—no, father—of your wife." However, he answered in the affirmative the query "Did you have a brother who went away several years ago?" admitting that he had not heard from him in several months. Phinuit said that Lodge would receive a communication from his brother in the near future. This prediction did not come true.

At Lodge's request, Phinuit tried to locate the brother. "A-f-Africa." "No." "A-m. Aus-austra—what you call Australia." The physicist said that his brother had once been in Australia. Not until later did he learn that his brother was then living in America. This news did not come through the medium.

Lodge had told Mrs. Piper about his seven children when he met her in Liverpool. Phinuit correctly said that one of the scientist's sons had worms and suggested vermifuge as a cure. Asked to name the boy's chief interest, the spirit control replied, "natural things; is musical." This was wide of the bull's eye. The son, Lodge noted, was intrigued by architecture. He drew housing plans and enjoyed books about buildings. Dr. Phinuit endeavored to indicate where there were marks and scars on the bodies of Lodge's progeny. These remarks were "not sufficiently precise to be useful information," the physicist wrote later.

Throughout the séance the spirit guide asked more questions than the sitter. "Have you got a George, J–O–R–G?" "No." "Who does Arthur belong to? You?" "No." Dr. Phinuit then said that Arthur was a member of the family of Myers, who had been taking notes behind a curtain and in whose home the medium was a guest.

Phinuit continued to fish for clues about the Lodge children: "You call one Charles." Lodge denied this. Phinuit persisted: "It's spelt with a C." Here Lodge gave, rather than received, information. "I have got a brother Charles, but never mind about the children, they are too many, and I get confused about them often myself." He was more interested, he said, in hearing about his other relatives, specifically his mother. No confirmable data about this parent were revealed. Dr. Phinuit asked more questions: "Who is Elizabeth?" There was no answer. "You have a great many relatives." "That's true."

The séance was almost over when the episode which Lodge called "the most striking and impressive" occurred. Phinuit mentioned the name Anne. Though he spelled it omitting the E, he identified her as an aunt, now dead, a sister of Lodge's mother, and the "best influence of his life." Aunt Anne had "looked after" him; "if you were in trouble, it pained her." Did Lodge have "a little old-fashioned picture of her, on a small card?" "Yes."

Aunt Anne said that she had the baby. "What baby?" Lodge asked. Aunt Anne replied, "I don't know, it's one of yours— a girl—a little thing; no, wait a bit, that's wrong—the girl's in the body; it's a little boy in the spirit she's looking after. There are two, a boy particularly. I don't see the other much."

Annotating the transcript of the séance, Lodge wrote that he had been unsure of the sex of his two dead infants until he had examined the medical records and found that both had been boys.

Phinuit said that the spirit of the aunt made him weak,

"tickling in the throat and breast (feeling all over her chest and mine) bronchial trouble, a little asthmatic—pneumonia, a little husky when she talks to me. . . . A trouble here (feeling chest and stomach), a trouble in stomach, and at last passed out with that illness, inflammation."

This was "practically true," Lodge noted, "except that the immediate cause of death was an operation for cancer in the breast. The nature of the pain was indicated to me more clearly by the graspings and hand indications of Dr. Phinuit on Mrs. Piper's body than by his words."

You may wonder why Lodge and, earlier, James had been so amazed. Mrs. Piper's séances were emotion-charged performances. Only those who sat quietly as she went through the throes of entrancement and then began speaking in a voice quite different from the one that she used in everyday conversation could appreciate the effect this created. It was as though another soul had taken possession of her body. If, as often happened, names were called that had no significance to those present, believers had a ready explanation: More than one spirit force was trying to break through.

With few exceptions, those who attended the séances were there because they hoped to communicate with the dead. William James had not attempted to record word by word what was said at the first sittings he had attended. Even later, he made only occasional notes while in the medium's presence. Fortunately, the investigators in England were often more precise.

Members of the Society for Psychical Research familiar with the methods of professional thought readers suggested that as the medium held Lodge's hands, she could tell by his unconscious muscular reaction whether he accepted a statement or rejected it. There was general agreement that a newcomer's first sitting with Mrs. Piper was the one to be studied most carefully. Information disclosed in one way or another at the initial encounter was often repeated and used effectively in later sittings.

The notes made by the Reverend Thomas Lund, chaplain of the Liverpool School for the Blind, were published in

the sixth volume of the English psychical research society's
Proceedings, along with the reports of Mrs. Piper's first series
of sittings in Britain and comments by other participants.

"What impressed me," Lund wrote, "was the way in which
she seemed to feel for information, rarely telling me anything
of importance right off the reel, but carefully fishing, and
then following up a lead. It seemed to me that when she
got on a right track, the nervous and uncontrollable movement of one's muscles gave her the signal that she was right
and might steam ahead."

During the séance Dr. Phinuit said, "You had a fire a little
time ago—no—a long time ago. Some little thing got burnt."
At first he called the object a drapery, then a tapestry, and
eventually correctly specified a rug. The spirit control called
the chaplain by name, but Professor Lodge's wife had addressed him by his surname within hearing distance of the
medium before the séance.

At one point Phinuit had said, "Who is it you call Lira
. . . Eleanor, Caterina, a sister, two names—one's Emma,
a sister, connected with you through marriage? Do you know
Thomas?" The chaplain answered the last query with, "I'm
Thomas." With this lead an alleged spirit sister, communicat-
ing through the medium, said, "He'll know me—Thomas
Lon—Lund—Thomas Lund."

The high point of the session, Lund wrote, was the correct
reference to a young sister, Maggie, and the name she was
sometimes called by at home, Margie. However, to get Maggie, Lund noted, the spirit control "went through a long
list." Dr. Phinuit correctly said that the chaplain had grieved
for his sister "all his life," and that he was a "long way off
when she died." "Ask her why I wasn't here," the chaplain
pressed. The voice that came from the medium replied, "I'm
getting weaker now—*au revoir.*"

Lund was told, during a later sitting, "that I was studying
for a degree, and had an illness, and that was why I was
not there when my sister passed out." This, he noted, was
not true. At another séance Dr. Phinuit described the Reverend Lund as "a very hard man" and visualized him as a

preacher "yelling away for all he's worth." As to his style in the pulpit, Lund commented that "nothing could be a more ludicrous caricature than this last."

The chaplain's opinion of Mrs. Piper's trance verbiage: A blend of facts and falsehoods, some meaningful, some absurd. More "careful testing" would be required to convince him that she had been in a trance, that telepathy had been involved, or that she had been in touch with spirits.

In *The Evidence for the Supernatural*, published in London in 1911, Dr. Ivor L. Tuckett, a physiologist, presented a thorough critical analysis of the printed reports on Mrs. Piper's trance phenomena. Neither thought transference, spirit aid, fishing questions nor muscle reading supplied the medium with some of the names she had accurately mentioned in trance. Professor Lodge's wife had called Chaplain Lund by his surname within earshot of Mrs. Piper. Other sitters also had provided information. Not until one of them, Mrs. A. W. Verrall, casually mentioned her daughter Helen's name in conversation with the medium did Dr. Phinuit speak it during a trance.

Professor Lodge confessed in the *Proceedings* that though he had introduced another sitter, E. C. Conner, under an assumed name, "I accidentally used his right name once in Mrs. Piper's presence." Dr. Walter Leaf, reporting on the medium's sittings in and around London, wrote that W. A. Pye "had been previously introduced as Mr. Wilson, but his real name had accidently been mentioned before Mrs. Piper. It is, however, extremely improbable that she heard it." Leaf also noted that his wife was not called Rosie until she had been addressed by this name "before Dr. Phinuit, as well as Mrs. Piper."

According to the *Proceedings,* "perhaps the most successful and convincing" séances given by the American medium on this visit to England were those for a woman referred to as Miss X. Unfortunately, Dr. Phinuit's statements were for the most part "of so private and personal a nature that it was impossible to publish them." We are told, however, that Miss X was also a medium and that Dr. Phinuit endorsed her.

It would have been equally instructive had a transcript of two of Mrs. Piper's sittings with another unidentified woman, Miss Z, been printed. This woman "was mourning for a near relative" and "gave so many hints that Mr. Myers, in the course of taking notes, guessed more of the facts than Phinuit succeeded in giving."

The men who paid Mrs. Piper's expenses and séance fees in England agreed that the medium was honest, that her trances were genuine, and that Dr. Phinuit fished and guessed for information. Still, the spirit doctor sometimes produced data seemingly beyond normal knowledge. Soon after the medium's return to Boston, her British sponsors arranged for Dr. Richard Hodgson, their representative, to continue to supervise most of her sittings and to send them comprehensive reports. For her services to the society Mrs. Piper was to receive an annual fee of approximately two hundred pounds.

Attempts to find evidence that a Dr. Phinuit had lived in the cities he had mentioned in France failed. Some researchers thought that he was a secondary personality of the medium; others supposed that Mrs. Piper had supernormal access to her sitters' thoughts and to those of living and dead people related to her patrons. The medium herself was willing to be tested until the source of her information could be determined.

She read the British *Proceedings* and discussed the various theories of the investigators with Dr. Hodgson. While she was entranced, Dr. Phinuit listened to him read the notes he had made at previous sittings and offered comments that clarified undecipherable words and phrases.

A new Piper communicator from the afterlife came through in Arlington Heights in 1892. George Pellew (called George Pelham or G. P. in the records) died in New York City in February. The thirty-two-year-old author had studied law at Harvard University before winning acclaim among his contemporaries as a philosopher with provocative ideas. His wide range of interests included psychical research. He had been an associate member of the Boston investigative society and once had attended a Piper séance under an assumed name.

Richard Hodgson remembered a discussion he had had with Pellew about the survival of personality after death. Pellew did not believe that this was possible. However, if he could return as a spirit and Hodgson was still alive, Pellew promised to "make things lively."

Less than five weeks after Pellew's burial the alleged voice of the dead doubter was heard at a Piper séance. Two sitters were with the medium—Hodgson and a younger man who had been a close friend of the deceased. When the friend removed a stud from his shirt and passed it to the medium, G. P. said, "That's mine. . . . I sent that to you." "When?" "Before I came here." The stud had been Pellew's, but it had been given to the friend by Pellew's father after his death.

The advent of G. P. ushered in a new phase of the Piper mediumship. Dr. Phinuit still spoke through the medium, but G. P. took control of her right hand as it wrote with a pencil on a pad. When names were spelled out, they were usually more accurate if a sitter held the hand by the wrist. (Tactile contact, it should be noted, enabled proficient muscle readers such as Washington Irving Bishop, Stuart Cumberland, and Alfred Capper to write words and numbers thought of by volunteer subjects.)

On a few occasions, at Dr. Hodgson's request, Dr. Phinuit spoke while G. P. wrote with one of Mrs. Piper's hands and another spirit controlled the other. During the early years of his investigation Hodgson had doubted that the medium's messages came from the dead. Now he believed that this was the only sensible explanation. G. P. recognized the sitters whom he had been acquainted with while he was alive and never claimed to know a person whom he had not met, Dr. Hodgson reported in the thirteenth volume of the British *Proceedings*.

The fact that G. P. did not always answer questions accurately did not disturb Dr. Hodgson. He reasoned that the memories of the dead were not as reliable, after the traumatic dying experience, as they had been when the consciousness was in the body. Further, it seemed logical that the dead would have difficulties getting their messages through from the other side.

Asked to explain the nature of a society that he and three ladies had formed two years earlier, G. P., "obviously confused," said, "development." Dr. Phinuit broke in with the word "Theosophic." Neither answer was correct. Then an attempt was made to name the members, "Helen Dering—Derrick, or Herrick." Even Dr. Hodgson admitted in the *Proceedings* that "the answer must be called wrong, although Helen was the first name of one of the members."

Two days later, during another sitting, G. P. claimed that he knew the names of the founders of the group, but as another sitter also did, he might be accused of reading her thoughts. He said that he would identify the ladies for Dr. Hodgson when they were alone. Hodgson's appended note in his report reads: "Many will regard this as perhaps an excuse for ignorance, as names subsequently given were not correct."

Most of the people who visited Mrs. Piper were as astonished as Professor William James and Dr. Hodgson had been by her trance revelations, but there were exceptions. After participating in a séance at James's home in Cambridge, Dr. S. Weir Mitchell wrote to James from Philadelphia on January 27, 1894, "If I had never seen you and heard your statements in regard to Mrs. P., my afternoon sitting with her would have led me to the conclusion that the whole thing was a fraud and a very stupid one. . . . On re-reading your notes I find absolutely nothing of value. None of the incidents are correct, and none of the very vague things hinted at true, nor have they any kind or sort of relation to my life, nor is there one name correctly given."

Professor James Mark Baldwin, who in September came from Princeton to assess a sitting at Professor James's invitation, found "three elements of truth" in the messages that Mrs. Piper delivered: Certain circumstances had been described about the life of one of his brothers; she had correctly said that another brother had died as a baby; his wife's initials had been called out after the medium had held a seal given him by his wife.

"The elements of truth were, however, so buried in masses of incoherent matter and positive errors . . . that the sense of her failure on the whole is far stronger with me." Professor Baldwin was not sure that the medium had been in a trance. "I am only disappointed that she did not give me more data for forming a positive opinion."

Another of Professor James's academic associates, Professor Herbert Nichols, who lectured at Harvard, wrote the psychologist that he had had "a wonderful sitting with *Mrs. Piper.* . . . She is no fraud. . . . She is the greatest marvel I have ever met. I am now wholly convinced." Though he had "asked her scarcely a question, . . . she ran on for three-quarters of an hour, telling me names, places, events in a most startling manner."

Most of the information was too personal to repeat in a letter. He could mention one incident. His mother had given him a ring with "the *first word* of his favorite proverb" engraved in it; he had given her a similar ring bearing the first word of the proverb she liked best. He had lost his ring, but had received hers after her death. He held this ring in his hand and concentrated on the inscription.

"What was written in Mamma's ring?" Professor Nichols asked the entranced medium. Immediately she wrote something on a piece of paper. Though this was not the word inscribed on the ring in his hand, it was the one on the ring he had lost.

John Trowbridge, a noted Harvard physicist, brought a handkerchief that a brother of his wife had purchased for her thirty-five years earlier in India. She was the only person who ever touched it. Mrs. Piper did not tell the professor anything about the handkerchief or its owner. Still, Professor Trowbridge had been "struck by a sort of insane cunning in the groping of the woman after something intangible."

Geologist Nathaniel Southgate Shaler got the impression that the medium was honest. On the other hand, Dr. Phinuit, her spirit control, seemed to be a "preposterous scoundrel."

Until every possibility of deceit had been excluded, Professor Shaler said, investigators could make no progress.

Mathematician James Mills Peirce's sitting, as reported by Dr. Hodgson in the thirteenth volume of the *Proceedings,* had been "practically a complete failure. . . . Much that was said was wrong and what was right appearing to the sitter to be probably derived from indications given by himself." Professor Peirce himself added that he had not seen or heard anything that conveyed the idea that messages came from the dead. "No personal trait, no familiar and private sign, no reminiscence of old affection, no characteristic phrase or mode of feeling or thought, no quality of manner was there, to make the presence of a departed spirit seem real." Many names had been mentioned. Some he recognized; others were unknown to him, but not for a second did he feel that anyone but the medium had been speaking.

The greatest effort to verify statements uttered by Mrs. Piper while entranced was made by Anthony J. Philpott, a Boston *Globe* reporter. In his book *The Quest for Dean Bridgman Connor,* Philpot told how he became involved in a long and expensive search for a man who the medium said had been captured by brigands. Informed in 1895 that his son, Dean, an electrician, had died and been buried in Mexico City, W. H. Connor, a Burlington, Vermont, assistant postmaster, had a vision. In it Dean revealed that he was still alive and that another man had been buried in the grave. The vision was so vivid that the elder Connor described it to a friend, P. C. Dodge. Dodge repeated the story to the Reverend Minot J. Savage, a prominent member of the Boston psychical research society.

Through the minister, Dodge met Dr. Richard Hodgson, who arranged for him to have a sitting with Mrs. Piper. Dodge brought along a picture of the hospital where, according to the American consul in Mexico City, the young man from Vermont had died. The medium held the picture, and her spirit control confirmed the elder Connor's psychic impressions. Dean Connor was not dead. He was a captive in Dr. Gintz's lunatic asylum near Pueblo.

Dodge traveled to Mexico City and had the corpse exhumed. The hair was much darker than Dean's had been, and a New England doctor attested that the teeth were not those of his former patient. The Boston *Globe* sent reporter Philpott to Mexico to make a thorough investigation and, if possible, to find and rescue the missing American.

The American consul testified that he had sent W. H. Connor news that his son was dying of typhoid fever and that he had received money for the medical expenses. The consul also said that he had reported the death of the patient to his parents.

The body had not been embalmed and shipped to the United States because embalming costs were exorbitant in Mexico—$2,000—and because he was sure that the father would not want to pay this amount. The consul had been present at the funeral; the body was interred in grave 559 at the American cemetery in Mexico City.

The physician and the nurse who had been at Dean Connor's bedside during his final ordeal were no longer at the American hospital. The reporter learned that the nurse had married and was living in another Mexican city. He found the former Helen Smith, now Mrs. F. U. Winn, in Tuxpan. She testified that Dean Connor's hair had been lighter before he died, and said that the hair of typhoid fever victims frequently became darker as a result of the disease. Physicians in the United States confirmed this opinion.

A bone in the left ring finger of the corpse in grave 559 had been fractured; Dean Connor had injured this finger as a boy. A trip to Pueblo established that there was no institution for the mentally ill in or near the city. There also was no record of a Dr. Gintz there or in Mexico City.

A long summary of Philpott's report appeared in the March 21, 1897, issue of the New York *World.* Dr. Hodgson did not accept the reporter's conclusions. "If I had the means," he said, "I would go to Mexico and find Connor alive." The Boston *Globe* volunteered to pay his expenses, but he refused the offer. Hodgson had other preoccupations; new and intriguing spirit controls were taking possession of Mrs. Piper's body during her sittings. He had prepared another massive report on the one medium he trusted and had been asked to return to London and give a personal account to the Society for Psychical Research covering the ten years he had spent observing her trance manifestations.

After twelve years as Mrs. Piper's principal control, Dr. Phinuit spoke for the last time in 1897; he said that he had been assigned to other duties in the afterlife. His departure may have been hastened by the adverse publicity that the medium had been receiving as a result of her participation in the Dean Connor case. The French physician was replaced by a group of spirits which had dominated the séances of the Reverend William Stainton Moses, a British medium, until his death in 1892.

Dr. Hodgson urged Mrs. Piper to cooperate with those powerful forces, and G. P. vouched for them while she was entranced. Five years after Moses's death he and his guides began communicating through the Boston medium. Dr. Hodgson was aware that only the Reverend Moses had known the real names of Imperator, Rector, Doctor, and the other intermediaries that he had used to get in touch with those on the other side of death. Now, perhaps, their true identities could be established.

Unfortunately, neither Moses, when speaking through Mrs. Piper, nor any of his spirit guides gave their actual names, which, it was later found, he had written in a notebook before his death. Imperator had admitted that he was Malachi, a prophet who lived several centuries before Christ. Rector was the assumed name of Hippolytus, an early Christian bishop. Doctor purported to be Athenodorus, a Stoic philosopher.

Since Mrs. Piper generally wrote, rather than recited, messages from these distinguished men of ancient times, her task was less complicated that it would have been had she attempted to assume their voices and mannerisms. Also, in the intervening centuries the long-dead figures had mastered English.

Dr. James Hervey Hyslop, professor of ethics and logic at Columbia University in New York, had attended a Piper sitting in 1892 and had met her when it was over. Having thereafter followed the medium's work in the *Proceedings*, he was eager to see her again. This time he arranged a visit under test conditions. He went from Boston to Arlington Heights in a "closed" coach and covered his face with a mask before he left the conveyance and approached the medium's front door.

Dr. Hodgson welcomed him as "Mr. Smith" and then introduced him to Mrs. Piper. Dr. Hyslop bowed silently and did not shake hands nor utter a word, he wrote in his book *Science and a Future Life* (1905). He sat behind the medium and to her right, close enough to put her writing hand back on the pad when it went beyond the edges. Otherwise he did not touch her. Dr. Hodgson read and recorded what the spirit control wrote, and jotted down the words spoken by himself and the masked sitter.

Hyslop found the first part of the test séance unsatisfactory, "without incidents that were conclusive at the time for anything supernormal." Then the hand wrote "Charles," identified this as the sitter's brother, and reported that he had died of typhoid fever one snowy winter. Hyslop later confirmed that his four-and-a-half-year-old brother had died in March 1854, and that there had been snow on the ground. The cause, however, had been scarlet fever and measles.

The names Elizabeth and Mary, who was identified as an aunt, appeared next on the pad. Allen or Ellen followed, indicating some connection with Mary. The latter, Hyslop suggested, was perhaps an effort to get the name McClellan, as he did have an Aunt Mary who was the mother of a McClellan who had died. Possibly Elizabeth was a try for Eliza, "the name of my aunt by my mother's side and this McClellan's aunt by marriage of his stepmother."

Robinson, another name, meant nothing to Dr. Hyslop at the time. After other sittings, he came to think it a reference to himself as Robert's son, as that was his father's first name.

Diligently seeking explanations for the medium's failures,

he learned that several unfamiliar names written in association with the spirit of a woman who said that she was his
mother were correct and that other claimed relationships
were accurate—not for himself, but for someone he had met.

Subsequent sittings convinced Dr. Hyslop that Mrs. Piper
was beyond suspicion and that she did communicate with
the dead. Dr. Hodgson had held this view for several years;
now he admitted it openly. William James, in the August
24, 1898, issue of the New York *Herald,* observed that the
distinguished investigator's acceptance of spiritualistic phenomena "marks a critical passage in the history of the Society
for Psychical Research as well as in Dr. Hodgson's own career."

Professor James described the phenomena produced by
the Boston medium as "the most baffling things I know. Any
definitely known form of fraud seems out of the question;
yet undoubtedly, could it be made plausible, fraud would
be by far the most satisfying explanation, since it would have
no further problem outstanding. The spirit hypothesis exhib-
its a vacancy, a triviality and incoherence of mind painful
to think of as a state of the departed."

For three more years Leonora Piper submitted to the supervision of Dr. Hodgson—even her private clients could
have appointments only with his approval—then she rebelled.
Her complaints, published in the New York *Herald* on October 20, 1901, created consternation on both sides of the
Atlantic. After fourteen years as an "automaton," Mrs. Piper
announced that she had severed her ties with the scientists
who had controlled her. She had undergone their tests to
find out for herself whether she was "possessed or obsessed."
At first "the thought of making it a remunerative occupation
never occurred to me, although since then I have, as a matter
of fact, done so."

Professor William James, she continued, became interested
in her when "her maid of all work told a friend who was a
servant in the psychologist's home that I went into 'queer
sleep', that I was what is called a psychic, and he took steps

to make my acquaintance." He was responsible for her investigation by the Society for Psychical Research.

Early in her career, when she became entranced, "it was attended with something of a struggle. At first, I said disconnected things—it was all gibberish, nothing but gibberish. Then I began to speak some broken French phrases. I had studied French two years, but did not speak it well."

Later, Mrs. Piper explained, she "wrote automatically through G. P. about a certain famous man called, in the Society for Psychical Research reports, Mr. Martz. I do not see how anybody can look on all that as testimony from a person in another world. I cannot see but that it must have been an unconscious expression of my subliminal self writing 'such stuff as dreams are made on'." She asserted that in the reports "there is *no* evidence of sufficient scientific value to warrant acceptance of the spiritistic hypothesis." She had never thought of herself as a spiritualist. She did "not believe that the spirits of the dead" talked through her while she was entranced.

This outburst by the woman generally accepted as the most reliable trance medium in the world threatened to demolish the strongest case ever recorded for a mental psychic. Then the storm clouds dissipated. Dr. Hodgson was quoted in the October 26, 1901, issue of the *Westminster Gazette:* "Mrs. Piper had not discontinued her sittings for the society. . . . The statement made by her represented simply a transient mood." A day earlier, in the Boston *Advertiser,* the medium herself claimed that she had been misquoted. "Spirits of the departed may have controlled me and they may not. I confess I do not know."

William Piper, her husband, died in 1904. A year later, in December, Dr. Hodgson dropped dead while playing handball at a Boston boat club. In *The Story of Psychic Science* (1930), Hereward Carrington wrote that during Dr. Hodgson's last years no one was permitted inside his small room on Charles Street. The skeptic of other days had become such a devout believer that he received personal messages there from Rector, Imperator, and other spirit communicators. Another live person might disturb the delicate atmosphere. According to Carrington, the respected investigator thought that "his critical acumen and judgment" would be questioned if his secret rites became known.

After Dr. Hodgson's death in 1905, the Boston organization, which had been founded as the American Society for Psychical Research in 1885 and converted into the American branch of the London society in 1889, disbanded. The present American Society for Psychical Research was established in 1907 by Dr. Hyslop, who became the principal American investigator of the Piper phenomena. Dr. Hodgson, however, continued to attend the séances—as a spirit.

Leonora Piper had known Hodgson for eighteen years, and during that time he had arranged most of her sittings. Now the Hodgson control that wrote and spoke while she was entranced was by far her most convincing trance characterization. This was confirmed in William James's report on this phase of the Piper mediumship in the third volume of the *Proceedings* of the new American Society for Psychical Research and in the twenty-third volume of the English *Proceedings*.

On December 28, 1905, a week and a day after Dr. Hodgson's death, the words "Hodgson—I am" were written by the medium's right hand. "Is this my friend?" the sitter, Theodate Pope, asked. Mrs. Piper's hand struck the pad five times, apparently an affirmative answer. Less than a week later, a longer message came through: "RICHARD HODGSON I AM WELL HAPPY GLAD I CAME GOD BLESS POPE." This was followed by an eight-line poem.

A ring, given to Dr. Hodgson as a fiftieth birthday present by a woman called Mrs. Lyman in the report, had been, he claimed in January, taken from his finger and kept by the undertaker. At a sitting in March, however, Hodgson recalled removing the ring himself and putting it in his vest pocket at the boat club. Someone there had stolen it. More than two months later the spirit described the man who had taken the ring from Hodgson's locker and said that the thief lived on the third floor of a "five-story brick house not far from the club." Eventually the ring was found; it was in Hodgson's vest at the home of a friend, George Dorr. Dorr did not match the description of the thief, and his house was not near the club. During the interim Dorr had talked with Hodgson at Mrs. Piper's sittings, and the ring had not been mentioned. He had not known that it was in the vest pocket until he came across it by accident.

The Hodgson control delighted many of the people who had been friends of the investigator. He reminisced about the good times they had enjoyed together and spoke or wrote words he had often used while living. On January 23, 1906, when Professor James's wife and William James, Jr. were the sitters, the Hodgson voice greeted them: "Why, there's Billy! Is that Mrs. James and Billy? God bless you! Well, well, well, this is a good." Hodgson's words often were so repetitious and stereotyped, noted Professor James, that they made "insipid reading," so he deleted many of them from his account. Another brief sample of a typical greeting will suffice.

"Well, well, well well! Well, well well, that is . . . Here I am. Good morning, good morning, Alice." "Good morning, Mr. Hodgson." "I am right here. Well, well, well! I am delighted!"

Like Dr. Phinuit, Hodgson did not have a high score on answering probing questions. Asked to give the names of his close friends at the Tavern Club in Boston, with whom he played pool and swam, Hodgson mentioned six men. One was not a member; the other five were not among his cronies.

The Hodgson evidence, Professor James wrote, was "vastly more leaky and susceptible of naturalistic explanation than is any body of Piper material recorded before. Despite this, he still believed that Mrs. Piper had a supernormal ability. "But if asked whether the will to communicate be Hodgson's, or be some mere spirit counterfeit of Hodgson's, I remain uncertain and await more facts, facts which may not point clearly to a conclusion for fifty or a hundred years."

On her second trip to England, in 1906–7, Mrs. Piper gave

more than seventy sittings. Her third visit, which extended from the fall of 1909 to that of 1911, was less productive. Illness brought on by a persistent cold hampered her psychic as well as her social activities. Several months before, she had written Anne Manning Robbins, an old friend in Boston, that she dreaded "the strain of scientific investigation again. I simply feel as though I could not do it possibly."

Miss Robbins, in her *Past and Present with Mrs. Piper* (1921), tells of the messages that she recorded over a period of thirty-two years at her sittings with the medium. One spirit communicant, Augustus P. Martin, a former Boston mayor and police commissioner, gave her a description of heaven. It was similar to a garden spot on earth, but without imperfections. The air was perfumed, and there was no night. Martin lived in a palatial mansion; his life was an idyllic version of the one he had lived on earth. He enjoyed making notes for his lectures, observing the beautiful flowers, watching the birds, and listening to music. From his window he could see fifty young musicians playing the same sort of instruments that had pleased him while he was in the flesh. He went to lectures by others, and they came to his. Following a few hours of prayer, which replaced rest and sleep, he was ready for another marvelous day. The late police commissioner (for whom Miss Robbins had worked), like Hodgson, sent back from the spirit world such greetings as "Well, well well!" and "Hello, hello, hello!" He advised Miss Robbins on business and personal matters and gave her information which she was sure the medium could not have learned from an earthly source. A few months after Dr. Hyslop, the secretary of the new American Society for Psychical Research, died in 1920, Miss Robbins's dead brother reported that he saw the investigator on the other side, "rushing about like a duck." Miss Robbins reported that Mrs. Piper, while in England, had perfected a method of writing spirit messages without going into a deep trance. She simply held a pencil, her eyes had a dreamy look, and she began to write. Rector and Dr. Hodgson were still her principal controls.

In her seventies, Leonora Piper was no longer as interested

in having investigators observe her sittings as she once had
been. One sitter had said in the early years that she reminded
him of an efficient nurse; now she had the air of a prosperous
matron. She wore glasses, except when ready to receive spirit
communications, and her hearing had deteriorated. Years
before, Dr. Phinuit had told sitters to address their questions
to the hand that wrote; now it was necessary for the words
to be spoken louder.

Dr. Gardner Murphy, later president of the American Society for Psychical Research, attended several Piper sittings
in 1924. Sir Oliver Lodge, Dr. Richard Hodgson, and Dr.
George Hervey Hyslop had been converted to a belief in
spiritism by the famous medium. Dr. Murphy, like Professor
William James, resisted the will to believe that the dead controlled her.

At the age of ninety-one, Mrs. Piper lived with her gray-
haired younger daughter, Minerva, in a Boston apartment,
Murray Teigh Bloom reported in "America's Most Famous
Medium," published in the May 1950 issue of the *American
Mercury.* She was "in surprisingly good health, although quite
deaf." Few of her neighbors who saw her walking with a
nurse remembered or knew about the stir she had created
at the height of her fame.

Mrs. Piper, in her public statements, always said that she
was not sure whether the dead spoke through her voice and
wrote through her hand. Before 1950 was over, if the spiritualistic hypothesis is correct, she had herself confirmed or
rejected the soul-communication theory in the afterlife.

16.

Reincarnation?

The thought of being born again after death with no option as to place—perhaps a jungle or a remote igloo in the polar region—or gender or social class is a disturbing one to most Americans and Europeans. Even more unsettling is the prospect of one or several lifetimes as a gnat, a poison ivy plant, or a clam. Yet, more people have accepted the reincarnation and transmigration tenets of Hinduism and Buddhism than have espoused Islamic, Judaic, or Christian doctrines.

To those who believe in it, a cycle of life in which the soul strives for perfection is as logical as the continuation of crops when seeds have been planted. A passage in the *Bhagavad Gita,* an ancient Hindu text, says that souls discard decrepit bodies as men throw aside tattered garments and don new clothes.

An Anglican prelate, Dean William Ralph Inge of St. Paul's Cathedral in London, considered the many-lives concept to be "credible and attractive." Some noted Americans expressed similar views, among them the poets Ralph Waldo Emerson and Walt Whitman, the inventor Thomas Alva Edison, the horticulturist Luther Burbank, and the automobile manufacturer Henry Ford.

Thinkers with a strong sense of personal identity shudder when contemplating the ultimate goal of Buddhism—the merging of individual awareness with a cosmic consciousness. Benjamin Franklin mused about the possibility of past and future lives, but unlike Empedocles, an early Greek philosopher, he did not recall former existences as a female, a male, a bird, a bush, and a fish.

Most psychical researchers shun reincarnation as a subject unworthy of scientific scrutiny. An outstanding exception is Dr. Ian Stevenson, Carlson Professor of Psychiatry at the University of Virginia School of Medicine and director of its Division of Parapsychology. Stevenson, the Canadian-born son of an Ottawa-based London *Times* correspondent, has collected, classified, and assessed more than sixteen hundred accounts of men, women, and children who remember previous lives. He himself has conducted extensive interviews in Asia and on the two American continents with people who claim to have lived in other times.

The sixty-year-old professor, with neatly trimmed, graying hair and dark-rimmed glasses, wears suits and ties as conservative as most of his published opinions. The title of his major book is carefully phrased—*Twenty Cases Suggestive of Reincarnation.* Published by the American Society for Psychical Research in 1966, it was corrected, revised, and expanded by the author before the University Press of Virginia reissued it in 1978.

As a boy, Stevenson read about reincarnation, and, at the age of nine, stressed the points in its favor to two women he met on shipboard while en route to England with his father. "I would call myself prematurely grave as a child," he confessed to Tom Buckley, who wrote an article about him in the September-October issue of the magazine *Quest/ 78.*

A graduate of McGill University School of Medicine in Montreal, Dr. Stevenson was working in New Orleans at Louisiana State University School of Medicine when a nationwide furor was created in 1956 by *The Search for Bridey Murphy,* a book about a Colorado woman who, while hypnotized, vividly recalled a past life in Ireland. Until then reincarnation had not intrigued the American public at large. Dr. Stevenson read the account carefully and marveled that a subject fascinating to him could have such wide appeal to the western world.

Bridey Murphy made best-seller lists two weeks after being published on January 1, 1956; in just twenty weeks, 205,500 copies were purchased. The book appeared in condensed form in *True,* a magazine, and more than fifty newspapers ran it serially. There was a British edition and versions in French, Spanish, Dutch, Italian, Swedish, Danish, and Finnish.

Author Morey Bernstein, a Pueblo, Colorado, businessman, had hypnotized Virginia Tighe (called Ruth Simmons in the book) as she stared at the flame of a candle. Told that she was a child of seven, the twenty-nine-year-old subject said, in response to Bernstein's questions, that she was at school in Chicago and named several classmates. Told she was five, she spoke of her friends in kindergarten. Then, as an infant, she talked about her doll, Baby.

Urged to go far back in time to a scene in a distant land, she said, again in response to the hypnotist's queries, that she was eight and lived in Cork, Ireland. The date was 1806, and her name was Bridey Murphy. She mentioned so many names and places while telling of her subsequent wedding and other events in Belfast that Bernstein tried to verify that this particular person actually had been born and had married and died in Ireland during the period specified by the entranced Mrs. Tighe.

According to the Chicago *Tribune,* the book took "the reader on a weird adventure through the most ponderous iron curtain of all—the human mind—and into the mysterious unknown realms of hypnotism." *Newsday* termed it "a tantalizing mystery story, a factual one, that will provoke and stimulate the reader and leave him wondering."

Bridey Murphy parties became the vogue. Guests attended garbed as they might have appeared in another existence as Cleopatra, Casanova, Anne Boleyn, or Henry VIII. Cartoons also reflected the craze. In one, an irate shopper informs a friend, "So then he started to call me Bridey Murphy. Said nobody could learn to cook as badly as I do in just one lifetime."

The Associated Press reported that a suicide note had been found near the body of a Shawnee, Oklahoma, newsboy, who had killed himself with a pistol. Richard Swink's message read, in part, "I am curious about this Bridey Murphy story, so I'm going to investigate in person."

Ernie Hill, a Chicago *Daily News* correspondent, spent three days in January 1956 in the region of Ireland described by Bridey Murphy without finding a single official document proving that she had lived there. William J. Barker, assistant editor of the *Empire* supplement in the Denver *Post*, probed in Ireland for three weeks. His twelve-page account of this investigation was published on March 11, 1956. He wrote engagingly of his search, but could not attest that Mrs. Tighe's Bridey had ever existed, except in her imagination.

A Chicago *American* series published that May and June, though more conjectural than substantive, unearthed some interesting information. As a youngster in Chicago, Virginia Tighe had lived across the road from a Mrs. Corkell. Mrs. Corkell had been born in County Mayo, Ireland; her first name was Bridie!

Denver *Post* feature writer Bob Byers asked Virginia Tighe about Mrs. Corkell. She remembered that she had played with her neighbor's children, but said that she had never heard Mrs. Corkell being called Bridie.

After a Bernstein hypnotic session, Mrs. Tighe had delighted him by dancing an Irish jig. The Chicago *American* noted that she had taken dancing lessons as a girl in Chicago. Asked about this by reporter Byers, Mrs. Tighe could not think of "anything specifically" that the instructor had taught her. Moments later she recalled the Charleston and the Black Bottom.

Byer's front-page story in the Denver *Post* of June 17 declared that the Chicago paper's charge that Mrs. Tighe tapped childhood memories had not been proven. *Life* on June 25 presented another opinion: "Last week *The Search for Bridey Murphy* was ended by a series of Chicago *American* articles."

The controversy, however, was far from over. When the Summer 1956 *Tomorrow,* a quarterly, posed the question "BRIDEY MURPHY—Fact, Fraud, or Fancy?", Dr. J. B. Rhine, the Duke University parapsychologist, answered that he did not find anything in the book "that the student of science would want to take seriously." Dr. Gardner Murphy, general research consultant of the Parapsychology Foundation, replied that he saw "no reason to believe that this book exemplifies a case of reincarnation." Dr. Geraldine Pederson-Krag, a contributor to the *Psychoanalytic Quarterly,* interpreted Virginia Tighe's statements as "the revelation of a fantasy which, consciously or unconsciously, the subject has been elaborating all her life."

The most devastating criticism came from Dr. Eric J. Dingwall, a British anthropologist who had conducted many investigations for the Society for Psychical Research. He listed the vital facts, according to Mrs. Tighe's own statements. Bridey had been born in 1789, one of the three children of a barrister who practiced in Cork. Her brother's wife was Aimee Strayne. Aimee's mother had a school and a stable. Bridey married Sean Brian Joseph McCarthy in Belfast in 1828. She had been to Father Gorman's St. Theresa's Church, near Dooley Road. According to Dingwall, no traces of "*any* of these persons" had been found. Nor could references to the school and stable in Cork or to Dooley Road in Belfast be located. There was a St. Theresa's Church, but only since the twentieth century.

Dr. Dingwall wondered why Mrs. Tighe had not been asked for the source of the Bridey Murphy tale while under hypnosis. Others wondered about this too. It became known that after the sixth session, she had refused to permit Bernstein to entrance her again. Nor, in the years since, has she allowed anyone else to hypnotize her. She is not interested in psychical research.

Dr. Ian Stevenson had followed the Bridey Murphy developments avidly. After *A Scientific Report on "The Search for Bridey*

Murphy," edited by Dr. Milton V. Kline, was published in 1956, he reviewed it the following January in the *Journal of the American Society for Psychical Research.* He felt then and does today that some of the statements made by Mrs. Tighe while entranced could not be explained away as bits of forgotten memories. He was quoted by Tom Zito in the November 18, 1978, issue of the New York *Post,* as saying that "Bridey, who had never been to Ireland nor knew anyone from there, spoke of a place in Cork called the Meadows. It's hard to explain where that bit of information could come from." Perhaps he had forgotten that Virginia Tighe admitted having known Mrs. Corkell who had been born there. As to the Meadows, Dr. Dingwall had commented that if Mardike Meadows, its proper name, had been given, this "statement might have been considered seriously."

Dr. Stevenson is skeptical about hypnotic-regression experiments generally. He prefers to study instances in which young children claim to be people who died before the children were born. The first of his *Twenty Cases* is Prakash Varshnay, who was born in Chhatta, India, in August 1951, a year and a half after the death of Nirmal Jain, the son of a prosperous merchant, in Kosi Kalan, a town some six miles away.

Months before his fifth birthday young Prakash had declared that he was Nirmal Jain and that his real home was in Kosi Kalan. He pleaded so often to be taken there that an indulgent uncle made the trip with him on a bus. Prakash did not recognize a store owned by Nirmal's father, possibily, Dr. Stevenson notes, because the shop was not open that day. Later he attempted to run away and begged so persistently for another visit that he was turned "counter-clockwise on a potter's wheel"—a tactic thought to erase disturbing memories—and then flogged. After this he no longer talked about his former life in the presence of his parents.

When Prakash was ten, Nirmal Jain's father, having heard about the youngster who claimed to be his reincarnated son, came to see him. Prakash identified the visitor as his father and, according to Dr. Stevenson, "partially recognized" the merchant's daughter. That is, the boy called Memo by her sister's name, Vimla.

On his second trip to Kosi Kalan, Prakash led the way to the merchant's house. There he identified several members of the family and indicated that he was familiar with their affairs. Less than three weeks after this dramatic confrontation, the American parapsychologist arrived on the scene. Dr. Stevenson spent two days investigating the case in 1961 and two more verifying details in 1964. His queries were posed and answered through interpreters.

While this case is suggestive of reincarnation to Dr. Stevenson, it is also suggestive of another explanation to the reader who studies the data provided by Dr. Stevenson. Did someone tell the child about the Jain family in the town six miles away? Did he go there before his second known trip and observe the people whom he later called by name? Is this theory more farfetched than the hypothesis of reincarnation?

As to the possibility that children who claimed to recall earlier lives in parts of the world where reincarnation is a widely held belief were visualizing themselves as members of more prosperous families, Dr. Stevenson said that in several of his twenty cases this was true. He had, however, studied other cases "in which the claimed previous life occured in less favorable circumstances than the present one."

Dr. Gina Cerminara, a psychologist who champions the many-lives cause, writes in *The World Within* (1957) that the theory of reincarnation "is really the scientific theory of evolution on a psychological and cosmic level." Several paragraphs later, however, she admits that there is no scientific proof of reincarnation.

To this psychologist, the Shanti Devi case, summarized in Morey Bernstein's Bridey Murphy volume, was the most convincing account of its kind. At the age of four Shanti, who lived in New Delhi, began talking about her earlier life in Muttra. Seven years later Shanti had so impressed three men in New Delhi that they arranged for her to go to Muttra. There she identified the man who, she claimed, had been her husband, astonishing him and others with her knowledge of events that had taken place twelve years earlier. Recalling that she had once buried money in the cellar of the Muttra house, she dug up a box. When opened, it was empty. The alleged husband confessed that he had taken the money after his wife's death.

Though none of Dr. Stevenson's *Twenty Cases* has such a dramatic climax, many are rich in recalled details. Gnanatilleka Baddewithana, a young girl in Ceylon, told about her memories as a *boy* in a town some sixteen miles distant. Her real father, she said, worked for the post office; a dog had bitten her brother; the train carrying Queen Elizabeth on her visit to Ceylon had gone through the town. The train that Gnanatilleka herself rode as a boy to attend school ran through a tunnel. The name of one of her brothers was Dharamadasa; Sudda Akka, a sister, traveled to Nawalapitiya for classroom instruction. The family house had a post office nearby on one side and, a short distance away on the other, a bus stop.

Although the house where she said that she had lived as a boy was no longer there, Gnanatilleka correctly indicated where it had stood. She called her alleged father and mother by name when she saw them, and identified a brother, two sisters, and several former acquaintances.

Such details are lacking in Dr. Helen Wambach's *Reliving Past Lives: the Evidence under Hypnosis* (1978). In an unspecified Quaker library in Mount Holly, New Jersey, in 1966 the psychologist felt impelled to reach for a book. (The title is not mentioned.) She opened it and saw a strange vision: She was astride a mule, reading the same book, which told of a clergyman hovering between life and death. Moments later she was back in the library with the book in her hand.

She wondered whether she had been fantasizing or whether she had been projected back into a past reality. It had taken her a decade and two thousand study sessions, Dr. Wambach wrote, to arrive at an answer. Not until the sixth page from the end of her book does she refer to her personal quandary again. If she had found an explanation, she did not mention it. In her words, "the answer is up to the reader."

Dr. Wambach conducts hypnotic age-regression seminars. Participants bring pillows and blankets and relax on the floor while Dr. Wambach, seated in a chair, lulls them to sleep hypnotically. When the subjects seem to be entranced, she instructs them to project themselves into the distant past. Target areas are such remote periods as 2000, 1000, and 500 B.C. and A.D. 25, 800, 1200, 1700, and 1850. The participants are told to remember how they were dressed, shod, and housed, and the food that they ate. After Dr. Wambach brings the time travelers back to the present, she tells them to describe their memories in writing.

One woman recalled a life as a man about two thousand years earlier. She wrote that she had lived near the Indian Ocean in a structure supported by poles. She had dressed in skins and eaten a custardlike breakfast food. A man remembering an existence in Babylonia at a similar period, described adobe dwellings. He had worn a long unadorned dress and sandals and had munched on cucumbers and cookies.

One peeker into the past said that she had been murdered; another had been stabbed. One man had been killed by an animal. A woman who had lived in Egypt when the Great Pyramid was being constructed had been beheaded, but didn't remember why.

Celebrants at Bridey Murphy costume balls in the 1950's had dressed as outstanding figures of bygone times—kings, queens, and other celebrities. The vast majority of Mrs. Wambach's subjects, in their various incarnations had been lower on the social scale—seamen, artisans, and homemakers.

A very small minority of the participants spoke of existences earlier in this century. One, named Anna, whom Dr. Wambach hypnotized in New Jersey, told of her experiences in Westfield, some fifty miles away. The time was 1917; her husband was a soldier; she had dealt in black market commodities and had committed suicide with a pistol. Dr. Wambach wrote down the name of the woman Anna claimed to have been, that of her husband, and other information imparted while the subject was entranced.

Here, at last, were data that could be checked and perhaps

provide evidence of another existence. The hypnotist went to Westfield. Issues of 1917 newspapers were available on microfilm. In them she found records of a druggist, a constable, and a police captain, all of whom Anna had mentioned. She found the grave of the man whom Anna claimed to have married, but no trace in the graveyard, or elsewhere, of a wife who had committed suicide.

How could Anna have known about people who had lived in another town before she was born without having lived there herself during this period? Almost grudgingly, Dr. Wambach gives a clue: Anna had an aunt in Westfield. And Anna, Dr. Wambach learned later, had lied about events in her current life: She had not been pregnant and had not had a miscarriage, as she claimed.

Another of Dr. Wambach's subjects, an older woman identified as Betty, recalled several existences over a period of five hundred years. She said that she had been a beggar in Pakistan, a barmaid in Britain, a Seminole infant in Florida, and James Buchanan, the fifteenth president of the United States. Some of Betty's memories as Buchanan were accurate; others were not. Dr. Wambach's subjects, she says, answer questions in the exact areas she specifies. In this case the hypnotist was more intrigued by Buchanan's private life than by decisions made while in office.

If there is any solid evidence that any of Dr. Wambach's subjects had a previous existence, this reader could not find it.

It is difficult to prove that anyone now living has had a previous existence. Unless a child who claims a past life has been observed by a researcher from the time this is first mentioned until the story is widely circulated several years later, there is always the suspicion that someone has coached him.

Dr. Stevenson has devised a test for those who think their personalities may persist after death. He proposed this survival test in the July 1968 issue of the *Journal of the American Society for Psychical Research.*

Stevenson asked people to send him combination locks which, if they followed his instructions, had been set so that only they, in another incarnation, or someone on earth to whom they have psychically transmitted the key numbers, will be able to open the locks. The lock he recommended is a sturdy one, Sargent and Greenleaf's Model 8088. Three turns of the dial will unfasten it, but those numbers must follow in sequence from the fifty possible markings on the revolving dial. This means the odds are 125,000 to 1 that any of the locks will be opened by accident or luck, there being 125,000 possible combinations.

In his reports on children who claimed past existences, Dr. Stevenson listed the many names, locations, and relationships that they allegedly recalled. In his *Journal* article, however, he points out that it may not be easy to remember six randomly selected digits after one has left the body, and he therefore tells how the first letters of the words in a six-word phrase or sentence can be converted into numbers.

Under the letters of the alphabet ten digits from one to zero are marked in sequence. The sequence is repeated when the letters *k* and *u* are reached. He cites an example—"We all certainly live after death." The initial letters of the words— WACLAD—are represented by the digits 313214.

Once a lock has been set, Dr. Stevenson says, it can be employed before the owner's death in tests for extrasensory perception. He has not as yet reported that anyone has succeeded in revealing the correct combination for any of the locks sent to him for safekeeping.

Another project designed to make future investigations of reincarnation easier was announced by Dr. Stevenson in 1971. In the summer *Newsletter* of the American Society for Psychical Research, he invited readers to write for a registration form on which they could give information about their present lives. He also welcomed such additional material as fingerprints, photographs, and recordings of voices. Among those who had sent data for his files were Chester F. Carlson, the inventor of xerography, and Professor C. J. Ducasse, the philosopher.

The response to this invitation was so overwhelming that Dr. Stevenson limited subsequent participants to men and women who had reached the age of sixty-five. Criticized for ignoring the reckless younger generation, one more likely to meet death suddenly and violently, the parapsychologist said that young people who were terminally ill would be included. He also was considering enrolling people in hazardous occupations—soldiers, police officers, "revolutionaries and gangsters."

Dr. Stevenson admits that he does not know what, if anything, passes from the dying to the newly born. He doubts that scientific proof of reincarnation will be presented in the foreseeable future. He ponders the cases he has investigated and is on the alert for new ones.

Efforts to document reincarnations, to see, weigh, analyze, and communicate with souls, and speculations about near-death visions all demonstrate that, even in a materialistic age, what occurs after death is still a paramount concern. Obviously, something—call it a soul, a divine spark, or a motivating force—is no longer present after a body dies.

It seems obvious to most people, if not to investigators of phenomena, that the search for the soul should begin at the time of conception or during the period of dying. This is when the animating power is generated or when it flickers and is finally extinguished. Instead, Sir William Crookes chose to probe the alleged powers of physical mediums, and Professor William James and Sir Oliver Lodge mused about the utterances of trance mediums.

There is no scientific proof of out-of-the-body experiences, yet the American Society for Psychical Research and the Psychical Research Foundation used part of the Kidd legacy to experiment with living subjects who professed to have the ability to detach their consciousnesses from their bodies. Collections of deathbed statments recalled by physicians and nurses are at best anecdotal evidence.

Future experimenters striving to discover the source of the soul and its destiny will be able, by analyzing the reports made by their predecessors, to see how preconceived ideas and the will to believe influenced the designs of investigation and led to a lack of proper precautions. Until every possible normal explanation of a supposed phenomenon has been eliminated, there is no ground to call a mysterious occurrence supernormal.

Meanwhile the soul continues to be, as some of the "primitive" peoples of the world have described it, as invisible as the aroma of a flower and as elusive as the wind.

Bibliography and Acknowledgments

Bernstein, Morey. *The Search for Bridey Murphy.* New York: Pocket Books, 1978.

Black, David. *Ekstasy: Out-of-the-Body Experiences.* Indianapolis and New York: Bobbs-Merrill Company, Inc., 1975.

Britten, Emma Hardinge. *Nineteenth-Century Miracles.* Manchester, England: William Britten, 1883.

Brown, Slater. *The Heyday of Spiritualism.* New York: Hawthorn Books, 1970.

Carrington, Hereward. *The Physical Phenomena of Spiritualism.* Boston: Small, Maynard & Company, 1908.

———. *The Coming Science.* Boston: Small, Maynard & Company, 1908.

———, and Meader, John R. *Death: Its Causes and Phenomena.* London: William Rider & Son, Limited, 1911.

———. *Personal Experiences in Spiritualism.* London: T. Werner Laurie Ltd., 1913.

———. *Modern Psychical Phenomena.* New York: Dodd, Mead and Company, 1919.

———. *The Problems of Psychical Research.* New York: Dodd, Mead and Company, 1921.

———. *The Story of Psychic Science.* London: Rider & Company, 1930.

————. *The Psychic World.* New York: G. P. Putnam's Sons, 1937.

————. *Laboratory Investigations into Psychic Phenomena.* Philadelphia: The David McKay Company, 1939. Reprinted in New York: Arno Press, 1975.

————. *The Invisible World.* New York: Beechhurst Press, Bernard Ackerman, Inc., 1946.

————. *Psychic Science and Survival.* New York: Beechhurst Press, Bernard Ackerman, Inc., 1946.

————. *Psychic Oddities.* London: Rider & Company, 1952.

————. *The Case for Psychic Survival.* New York: The Citadel Press, 1957.

Christopher, Milbourne. *Panorama of Magic.* New York: Dover Publications, 1962.

————. *Houdini: The Untold Story.* New York: Thomas Y. Crowell Company, 1969. London: Cassell, 1969.

————. *ESP, Seers & Psychics.* New York: Thomas Y. Crowell Company, 1970.

————. *Seers, Psychics and ESP.* London: Cassell, 1971.

————. *The Illustrated History of Magic.* New York: Thomas Y. Crowell Company, 1973. London: Peter Hale, 1975.

————. Mediums, Mystics & the Occult. New York: Thomas Y. Crowell Company, 1975.

————. *Houdini: A Pictorial Life.* New York: Thomas Y. Crowell Company, 1976.

————. *Geister, Götter, Gabelbieger,* Dusseldorf and Vienna: Econ Verlag, 1977.

————. *Milbourne Christopher's Magic Book.* New York: Thomas Y. Crowell, 1977.

Crookes, William. *Researches in the Phenomena of Spiritualism.* London: J. Burns, 1874.

Carrel, Alexis. *Man, The Unknown.* New York: Harper & Brothers, 1935.

Dingwall, Eric J. *The Critic's Dilemma.* Crowhurst, England: author's publication, 1966.

Ebon, Martin. *What's New in ESP?.* New York: Pyramid Books, 1976.

_____. *The Evidence for Life After Death.* New York: New American Library, 1977.

Fuller, John G. *The Great Soul Trial.* New York: Macmillan Company, 1969.

Green, Celia. *Out-of-the-Body Experiences.* New York: Ballantine Books, 1973.

Hall, Trevor H. *The Spiritualists.* New York: Helix Press, Garrett Publications, 1963.

_____. *Florence Cook & William Crookes.* London: Tomorrow Publications Limited, 1963.

Hardinge, Emma. *Modern American Spiritualism.* New York: author's publication, 1870.

Hendin, David. *Death as a Fact of Life.* New York: W. W. Norton & Company Inc., 1973.

Home, D. D. *Lights and Shadows of Spiritualism.* London: Virtue & Co., Limited, 1877.

Hyslop, James H. *Science and a Future Life.* Boston: Herbert B. Turner & Co., 1905.

_____. *Psychical Research and the Resurrection.* Boston: Small, Maynard and Company, 1908.

Kerr, Howard. *Mediums, and Spirit-Rappers, and Roaring Radicals.* Urbana, Chicago and London: University of Illinois Press, 1972.

The London Dialectical Society. *Report on Spiritualism, of the Committee of the London Dialectical Society, together with the Evidence, Oral and Written, and a Selection from the Correspondence.* London: J. Burns, 1873.

Mitchell, Edgar D. Edited by White, John, *Psychic Exploration.* New York: G. P. Putnam's Sons, 1974.

Moody, Raymond A., Jr. *Life After Life.* Covington, Georgia: Mockingbird Books, 1975.

_____. *Reflections on Life After Life.* New York: Bantam Books, 1977.

Medhurst, R. G.; Goldney, K. M.; Barrington, M. R. *Crookes and the Spirit World.* New York: Taplinger Publishing Company, 1972.

Moore, R. Laurence. *In Search of White Crows.* New York: Oxford University Press, 1977.

Murphy, Gardner, and Dale, Laura A. *Challenge of Psychical Research.* New York: Harper & Brothers, 1961.

———, and Ballou, Robert O. *William James on Psychical Research.* London: Chatto and Windus, 1961.

Osis, Karlis, and Haraldsson, Erlender. *At the Hour of Death.* New York: Avon, 1977.

Podmore, Frank. *Modern Spiritualism.* 2 vols. London: Methusen & Co., 1902.

———. *The Naturalization of the Supernormal.* New York and London: G. P. Putnam's Sons, 1908.

———. *The Newer Spiritualism.* London and Leipzig: T. Fisher Unwin, 1910.

Rogo, D. Scott. *Man Does Survive Death.* Secaucus, New Jersey: Citadel Press. 1977.

———, Ed. *Mind Beyond the Body.* New York: Penquin Books, 1978.

Robbins, Anne Manning. *Past and Present with Mrs. Piper.* New York: Henry Holt and Company, 1921.

Siwek, Paul. *The Enigma of the Hereafter.* New York: The Philosophical Library, 1952.

Stevenson, Ian. *Twenty Cases Suggestive of Reincarnation.* Charlottesville, Virginia: University Press of Virginia, 1978.

Swann, Ingo. *To Kiss Earth Good-bye.* New York: Hawthorn Books, Inc., 1975.

Tabori, Paul. *Pioneers of the Unseen.* New York: Taplinger Publishing Company, 1972.

Tart, Charles T. *Psi: Scientific Studies of the Psychic Realm.* New York: E. P. Dutton, 1977.

Tuckett, Ivor Lloyd. *The Evidence for the Supernatural.* London: Kegan Paul, Trench, Trübner & Co., Ltd., 1911.

Weiss, Jess E., Ed. *The Vestibule.* New York: Pocket Books, 1974.

Wilkerson, Ralph. *Beyond and Back.* New York: Bantam Books, 1977.

Wambach, Helen. *Reliving Past Lives.* New York: Harper & Row, 1978.

In addition to the books cited here and in the text many other volumes and documents in the libraries of the American Society for Psychical Research and the Parapsychology Foundation in New York City, the Society for Psychical Research in London, and the Harry Price Collection at the University of London were consulted.

For aid in various phases of the research I am indebted to Dr. Eric J. Dingwall and A. H. Wesencraft in England, and to Stephen Tigner, Canon William V. Rauscher, Martin Ebon, and Dr. Larkin Farinholt in the United States.

Unpublished manuscripts and letters of Hereward Carrington, Harry Houdini, John Mulholland, and other investigators in the author's collection were also sources of information.

Index